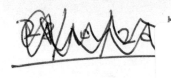

GET *I*

THE *REAL* SECRET OF SUCCESS REVEALED

Stay happy

Innocent

On Top Consulting Limited
36 Elthorne Road
Upper Holloway
London N19 4AG
Great Britain

www.ontopconsulting.co.uk

Published by On Top Consulting Ltd

First published 2002

© Dr Innocent A. Izamoje 2002

A catalogue record for this book is available from the British Library

ISBN 0–9543109–0-X

Design/Typeset by Saxon Graphics Ltd, Derby

Printed and bound in Great Britain by Cox & Wyman Ltd, Reading, Berkshire

GET *REAL!*

THE *REAL* SECRET OF SUCCESS REVEALED

by

Innocent A. Izamoje

Practical, tested and proven way to
succeed in life

On Top Consulting Limited

I dedicate this book to the loving memory of my dearly beloved successful late father, James Izamoje Echiejile, who was one person to the whole world, but the whole world to many a person.

CONTENTS

FOREWORD

... from the sky, from the earth, from a scrap of paper, from a passing shape, from a spider's web, ... We must pick out what is good for us where we can find it.

(Pablo Picasso).

Success is good for you and you will find the real secret of success in this book.

Although the sun shines on everyone, not everyone shines under the sun.

There are three aspects of life: getting in, getting on, and getting out. Everyone gets in and everyone gets out; but not everyone gets on. In life, we cannot change whether or not we are born or would die for everyone who gets in must get out.

But we can change and determine whether or not we GET ON with life and GET ON in life. The only way to GET ON is to GET REAL!

(Innocent Izamoje)

I have written this book to help you GET ON.

It is my hope and desire that you would get on with the book, grasp the real secret of success that it will reveal to you, and DO something with the secret in order to get on living life successfully and get on in various areas of your life.

Best wishes and God Bless.

Dr Innocent A. Izamoje
D.Phil; M.Sc; B.Sc (Hons.); MIMgt; FCIPD
London, United Kingdom.

ACKNOWLEDGEMENTS

It's the friends you can call up at 4am that matter
(Marlene Dietrich)

*The deepest principle in human nature is the craving to be
appreciated*
(William James)

I would like to appreciate and thank all those who contributed to the successful completion of this book.

Firstly, I thank God for saving my life after several near-death experiences and thereby made it possible for me to write this book.

I am grateful to my lovely wife – Gertrude – and to our two lovely sons – Chidi and Chinwe – for their valued support and inspirational comments that cheered me on and assisted me on the road to successfully completing this book. Additionally, I thank them for working together with me in ensuring the success and oneness of our family and for assisting me with thinking through various issues set out in this book.

I thank our lovely family friends – Adonna Kwabi and Mary Falese – for assisting me with the proofreading. I am very grateful to them.

I thank my lovely mother and my lovely brothers and sisters for their valued support and also for doing their own bit in ensuring the success and unity of our extended family.

I appreciate and thank the numerous people who have shared their knowledge and experiences with me on my various management and personal development training courses and seminars. I am also grateful to the numerous people who co-operated with me during my extensive research work and thereby enabled me to complete this book.

I thank you all very much.

INTRODUCTION

A journey of a thousand miles must begin with a single step.
(Lao-Tzu)

Success is a journey. This book would guide and assist you on your journey to success.

You may or may not have realised it, but by proceeding with studying this book, you have succeeded in making a bold decision and the right decision indeed. You have taken a crucial and helpful step on your journey to success. Congratulations!

Successful people make decisions and decisions make people successful.

Nobody can succeed in life without making the right decision including making a decision to succeed.

Life is about making choices and you have made the right choice to proceed with studying this book that reveals the real secret of success.

This book would teach you why some people succeed and others fail in life. It would also reveal to you the *REAL* secret of success and tell you what you must do in order to succeed and continue to succeed in life.

Like the sun that gives light to everyone, this book gives you real light by revealing to you the real secret of success that would enable you to shine in any area in which *you* personally *want* to succeed.

I wish you success. I also wish for you to continue to succeed and improve your own world and the wider world in which we all live.

May your success story be part of the evidence that would motivate and assist other people in our real world by helping them to succeed in life also.

Every road has a name just as every person has a name. **The road to success and the people who succeed in life have exactly the same nickname: TOUGH.** As you proceed on your journey of success, remember that the road on which you travel is tough, and that, as a tough person, you must NOT give up when the going gets tough. In other words, as you travel on the road to success, you must give up giving up!

In order to succeed in life, you must surely give up giving up. As H.W. Arnold reminds us, *the worst bankrupt is the person who has lost enthusiasm. Let one lose everything but enthusiasm and that person will again come through to success.*

Regardless of your past or current circumstances, when you get real and give up giving up, you would enthusiastically continue to press ahead, go for success and would definitely feel GREATER; that is:

Getting
Really
Enthused
About
Things
Everyday
Refreshingly

People who get real get really enthused about success everyday. They do not seek to succeed one day and then fail the next day. They know that success is a journey and in consequence, they seek to succeed everyday in a manner that is refreshing.

Like the sun, you really can shine and continue to shine with a refreshing sense of success everyday. If you or other people tell *you* that you cannot succeed as you proceed on your journey of success just get real with yourself or the other people and believe that you can and will succeed. An understanding of the real secret of success together with the proper application of that secret would enable you to succeed. Get real always and you would shine always.

In life, some conditions can be permanent. Success is a condition and you can succeed and permanently succeed when you permanently get real.

Enjoy your journey to success and the success of your journey.

1

LAST THINGS FIRST: WHY YOU NEED THIS BOOK

What we call the beginning is often the end. And to make an end is to make a beginning. The end is where we start from.
(T. S. Eliot)

Last things first! Therefore, let's begin with what you could get after doing what this book requires you to do.

Why should you buy a book, read it, or do what it tells you to do if you do not know what the book can do for you or for other people? Why should you spend your time, energy, money or other resources on something if you do not know what it could positively result in for you or for other people?

Successful people are not resource-wasters. They do not waste their time, money, energy, and other resources on things that do not or could not yield a positive result. Rather, successful people commit their resources to things that could yield a positive result.

Successful people who get real with themselves and the real world in which we live see the end of something before they begin doing it.

The end result of something motivates and enables them to start and then go through the process of attaining the result that they desire.

Be expectant! In order to succeed in life, you must expect to succeed. Successful people conceive and deliver their own success. This book is designed to enable, assist and guide you in the process of personally conceiving and attaining your own success.

You might have previously heard this saying: 'First things first'. This is true. But it is true only to the extent that it means that last things should come first. Although the result of an action normally comes at the end of the action, most people would tell you that it is what they expect to get from an action – the last thing – that is dominant (the first thing) in their minds even before they commence the action. Simply put, this means last things first!

Nothing is interesting if you are not interested in it. And to really become interested in something, real people need to know what's in that thing for them or for other people.

In order to succeed at anything, the first thing that you must do is to focus on the 'last' thing. You must know or visualise what the outcome of a process is or should be before starting the process. You should *see* or visualise where you are going to even before you start your journey. This is one of the important aspects of the real secret of success.

When you ask most people who pack their baggage and take their passports along with them to describe their intention to you, they would tell you they are going *to*, for example, Paris or New York (their destination) rather than the place – the airport – they are going *through*.

Success in life is about your destiny; namely, what or where you are going *to* as well as how you get there. It's not about what or where you are going *through*. You might go *through* a rough time and bumpy path on the road to success as everyone else does; but you must keep your *vision* with regard *to* where you are going in life.

What you want out of something, that is, the end result or the last thing, must be the first thing or the main thing in your mind when you commence an activity. **Successful people talk in 'outcomes' terms**. You too should have a vision and see the end of something before starting it.

Someone may be mixing sugar, eggs and other ingredients together. If you ask them what they are doing they would tell you they are making a cake. They focus on the end result – the visualized cake – rather than on what they were actually doing at the moment even if what they were doing at the time when you asked the question was simply mixing various ingredients together.

THE NEED TO SUCCEED

We all need to succeed in life. Although success does not come naturally, we all have a natural need to succeed in life. There is something in success for everyone. Similarly, there is something for everyone in understanding the real secret of success. In consequence, there is something for everyone in this book that reveals the real secret of success.

The word 'real' is used repeatedly in this book because the book deals with a real issue — success — for real people living in a real world.

As used in this book, the word 'REAL' does not present the real secret of success as though it is a single isolated thing or word. As you diligently study, work through, and understand every section of the book, the real secret of success would become revealed and apparent to you.

In a practical sense, the word 'REAL' is used in this book as a password. It is used as a key to unlock the door of your life and to open up avenues for you to succeed in life. The only known, tested, and generally applicable password for successful living is the word 'REAL'.

I have used the word 'REAL' as a password because it is a simple word that everyone is likely to remember as they seek and work towards achieving something that is real – success – in our real world.

Always remember the password to successful living – REAL – because you are living in a real world and success is real and there is a real secret to it. Always remember also that you can use a password to access something, for example, your computer; but when you gain access into the computer, the computer would not do anything for you if you do not do anything with it.

Therefore, be prepared to actually do something with this book because the book could do something for you only if you do something with it. Similarly, simply knowing the real secret of success that this book would reveal to you would be worthless to you if you do not do something with that real secret when it is revealed to you. In this book, I offer you the best thing you could ever get.

THE BEST THING YOU COULD EVER GET IN LIFE

If you give people fish, you feed them for the day; but if you teach people HOW to fish, you feed them forever.
(Chinese Proverb)

In this book, I offer you a gift; the best gift you could ever get in life! This book is a very different book. It was intended and written to be different so that it could make a positive and constructive difference in your life.

The best gift that people can give to each other is what I call the *HOW* gift:

His or Her
Own
Warrant

The *HOW* gift is designed to give you 'your own'. That is a powerful and refreshing point: *your own* success in whatever you are involved in. This is what this book can do for you: help you have your own warrant in life; your own success in whatever you are involved in.

In order to clarify that this book could give you the best gift in life, let us consider the real meaning of the word 'warrant'. There are many alternative words for the word 'warrant' including the following words: assurance, authority, authorization, commission, guarantee, licence, permission, permit, security, and warranty.

It is nice, isn't it, to have your own assurance, your own authority, your own guarantee, your own licence, your own … security and your own warranty in life! What better gift could someone give you than helping you to know HOW to have your own assurance, your own authority, your own … security and your own warranty in life? What better gift could you receive than knowing HOW to assure and secure your own success?

If you have a good knowledge of a particular subject, the best gift you could ever give to someone else is HOW to gain their own knowledge of the subject; if you have peace of mind, the best gift you could ever give to other people is to assist them with HOW they can have their own peace of mind; if you are a happy or relaxed person, the best gift you could ever give to someone else is HOW to secure their own happiness or relaxation. The list is endless. Overall, if you are a successful person, the best gift you could ever give to other people is to help them with HOW they could achieve their own success.

Undoubtedly, the HOW gift is the best and the most valuable gift of all gifts you could ever receive in life! In this book, I offer you the HOW gift. By offering you the HOW gift, I am putting in your hands a powerful and helpful tool with which you can cultivate your own success in life. I do not offer you success because success cannot be offered to you as a gift by anyone.

If indeed you can keep what you own and own what you keep, then the only thing in this world that you can both securely own and keep is your *HOW* tool; the tool that gives everyone:

> ## His or Her
> ## Own
> ## Warrant

When I was a teenager, I told my father that the most important thing I wanted in life was 'my own' not 'his own'. Rather than say in life that 'my father solves my personal problems for me', I wanted to grow up and say that 'I am able to and do solve my own problems myself'; rather than say that 'my father works hard and looks after me', I wanted to say as an adult that 'I work hard and look after myself'; rather than say 'this is my father's car' I wanted to say 'this is my own car'; and so on.

You should have your OWN. I constructed the abbreviation OWN as meaning **O**ngoing **W**ithout **N**ullification. The only way you can succeed, continue to succeed and really enjoy success in life is to have your own *HOW* gift that cannot be nullified or taken away from you by anyone and guarantees that you are continually moving forward and succeeding in life.

> *The only way to enjoy anything in this life is to earn it first.*
> (Ginger Rogers)

TESTIFY TO YOUR OWN PERSONAL SUCCESS

I was the Master of Ceremony at a recent social event in London. During the event, I asked the audience what they thought the abbreviation *MOT* meant.

As expected, they all replied that *MOT* meant 'Ministry of Transport'. In the United Kingdom, every vehicle must, in compliance with traffic regulations, have its own *MOT* Certificate in order to legally be on the road.

Different countries refer to the roadworthiness certificate for vehicles in different ways. For the purpose of my comparison, I would use the example of the United Kingdom where I currently reside to illustrate and substantiate the real point being made in this passage.

When my audience at the social event replied that *MOT* meant 'Ministry of Transport', I told them that the real meaning that I have personally attached to the label *MOT* as a certificate of roadworthiness that qualifies one to travel on the road to success in life is My Own Testimony.

Say this to yourself:

My
Own
Testimony.

Say it again:

My
Own
Testimony

In order to travel on the road to success everyone must have his or her own testimony. You must be able to testify to the things that *you* are personally *doing* to succeed in life.

Just as you cannot legally and rightfully use one vehicle's *MOT* certificate on another vehicle on a road in the United Kingdom – and the same principle applies in other countries – one person cannot legally and rightfully use another person's testimony on the road to success in life.

The road to success is not about other people's testimonies; it is about My Own Testimony. You must personally be roadworthy by having your own personal certification of the things that you are personally *doing* to succeed in order to successfully travel on the road to success. Everyone is the vehicle for driving his or her own personal success programme forward and everyone needs and must have his or her own *MOT* in order to travel on the road to success.

The point in the preceding paragraph was what I meant when I told my father that what I wanted in life was 'my own' rather than 'his own'. From a very young age, I knew that I would not be successful in life just because my parents were successful.

You would never be successful simply because other people are successful. Even if you inherit 'this or that thing' from other people, you must still DO your own 'thing' to successfully keep what you have inherited.

If you put one vehicle's *MOT* certificate on another vehicle in the United Kingdom – and elsewhere where the same principle applies – you would be breaking the road traffic law and the Government that made the law would duly punish you for that.

Similarly, if you do not have your own *MOT* on the road to success in life, you would be breaking a crucial natural law of life and would be duly punished by life. The only sensible response to this natural law that nobody can change – success does not come from human beings but from human doings – is to comply with it and ensure that you are personally *doing* things to succeed in life.

By asking you to seek your own testimony of the things that you are personally doing to succeed in life, I am not suggesting that you should not seek help from other people. Far from it! We all need help in various ways from other people. Seeking help is part of *doing* something to succeed. We can and should get the best out of our own world and the wider world around us.

Everyone can and should succeed in life. This book is designed to help you move forward rather than backwards.

You may have failed in the past; you may have been disappointed on many previous occasions; other people may have told you that you would not succeed in life; you may have told yourself and even convinced yourself that you would not succeed in life; there might be many examples that you or other people could point to about your past or current situations to indicate that you might not succeed in life; but yes, you can and should move on.

And yes, like many other people in the same or worse situation as you, you too can succeed by following the simple formula contained in this book.

And the only way that you can move on and then get on with successfully living life is to get real. When you get real, you must accept that everyone including *you* can and should succeed in various areas of their lives.

This book would challenge you to change and turn your story into a remarkable success story.

YOU ALONE CONTROL YOUR HOW GIFT

Your *HOW* gift cannot be taken away from you by other people because it is stored in your mind. Nobody can gain access into your mind without your permission. The only way you can lose your *HOW* gift is to lose your mind.

A crucial aspect of the real secret of success is associated with understanding how you can store success in your mind and then use your mind to create and retain success.

Other people should not take credit for your own success just because they told you *HOW* to achieve success. Many people might know how to achieve success in various areas of life but not everyone would be successful in various areas of life.

Someone can teach you and other people how to ride a bicycle but whether or not you all actually succeed in riding a bicycle is up to each person. What makes the real difference in whether or not you all actually succeed in riding a bicycle is not the how-to-ride-a-bicycle gift that was made available to everyone. Rather, it's *you* that make the real difference!

The preceding point is worth emphasising: What makes the real difference as to whether people succeed or fail is not the information that is made available to them. What makes the real difference is the application of the information by each person.

Similarly, whether or not everyone who reads and applies the principles taught in this book would succeed is very much up to the individuals concerned.

The approach adopted in this book is to reveal the real secret of success to you by offering you simple, tested, and practical principles and techniques that can enable you to create and retain your own success in any area of your life.

When you find the real secret of success in this book, just pick it out, permanently properly apply it and then enjoy your personal success.

2

WHY YOU MUST GET REAL

*Nothing in this world is so powerful as an idea
whose time has come.*
(Victor Hugo)

Nothing in this world is impossible to a willing heart.
(Abraham Lincoln)

Get real and succeed.
(Innocent Izamoje)

When you get real, you would know for sure that every successful thing that has been accomplished in our real world was once considered impossible.

A fact of life is that although we all *need* to succeed, not everyone *wants* to succeed because everyone does not GET REAL; and, in consequence, everyone does not actually succeed. Only people who consciously *want* to succeed and then GET REAL by *doing* things to succeed in life actually succeed. This is food for thought!

I would like to use the example of real food to further illustrate the real point being made in this passage.

Although we all *need* food in order to survive, not all of us succeed in having food let alone the kind of food we really need. In fact, although we all *need* food, some people consciously say they do not *want* food and then decide not to eat even when offered a free meal on a plate! There are many people who, for various reasons, go on hunger strike and do not want food even though we all really need food to stay alive!

Superficially, it might seem as though everybody *wants* to succeed in life. This is not true. **What is true about life is that everybody *needs* to succeed, but not everybody *wants* to succeed. The reason everyone does not succeed in life is simple: Not everyone combines a *need* with a *want*; and in consequence, not everyone fertilises his or her *need* to succeed by *wanting* to succeed.**

I use the word 'real' many times in this book to reflect the abbreviation *REAL*; namely, the:

 Ratified
Evidence
About
Life.

This book is based on clear evidence that is ratified or proven by something we all have in common: life.

People who get real fully understand and properly apply the Ratified Evidence About Life. Therefore, when I ask you to get real in this book, I am asking you to fully understand and properly apply to life, the Ratified Evidence About Life.

This book contains that evidence. Everyone must get real in order to succeed in life. This is a hard fact of life borne out by the Ratified Evidence About Life.

FAMILIARITY BREEDS CONSENT

Familiarity breeds consent in life. When you get real and become familiar with the real secret of success contained in this book, you, definitely, would consent to its practicality and usefulness. Through applying the principles that the book would teach you, you would be a welcome addition to the success stories in the world.

Although we are born with the *need* for something such as food, we must *want* it as well. People *do* something when they want to get what they need. Although we are born with a natural need to feed, we are not born with food. Similarly, although we are born with a need to succeed, we are not born with success. Success is not natural and it is not guaranteed to everyone.

Just as we must want to eat food in order to actually eat, we must also want to succeed in life in order to actually succeed.

I entitled this book 'GET *REAL*' because I want to offer people what is lacking in their lives rather than give them what they have already. We already have the *need* for success or the *need* to succeed in life.

Nobody goes to school because they need to fail at school or because they have a need for failing at school; nobody starts a business because they need to fail in business or because they have a need for failing in business; nobody gets married because they need to fail in their marriage or because they have a need for failing in their marriage; nobody goes into hospital because they need their health to fail or because they have a need for their health to fail; and so on.

Simply put, nobody has a *need* to fail! In all areas of life, everyone already has the *need* to succeed. What is lacking is that most people do not succeed only because they do not *want* to succeed. In other words, most people do not get real.

Some people might argue that they want to succeed but that the problem is that they just cannot succeed. This is not true. This book would use the Ratified Evidence About Life to demonstrate what it really means to WANT to succeed. The Ratified Evidence About Life presented in this book shows that people who really WANT to succeed and then *get real* would succeed.

You can succeed regardless of your background. Someone might tell you that nothing is guaranteed in life. That is not true. There are things that are guaranteed in life. For example, it is guaranteed that the sun would definitely rise and then set and then rise and shine again. Even if there were an eclipse of the sun, the sun would definitely shine again. Similarly, anything or anybody can eclipse your life but you can really shine again and again and you can shine always. You might experience a period of 'darkness' in your life, or like the sun, *you* might 'go down' but if you get real, you are guaranteed to rise and shine again.

You don't have to 'fall down'. Even when you 'go down', just remember that, like the sun, you would rise and shine again and that you would shine forever as long as you continue to get real.

When you get real in life you would definitely have a *place in the sun* and you would shine not just on your own personal world but also on the wider world around you.

As I write this passage, I have just looked outside through my window and the sun is shining out there. The light that the sun gives out there reminded me of something that I read on a vehicle in Nigeria when I was growing up as a young child: *No condition is permanent.*

When I was growing up as a young child in Nigeria, I noticed that many of the commercial vehicles especially the coaches and buses in Nigeria had very powerful motivational and inspirational statements written on them.

I used to like and had believed a statement on some of the buses and coaches that I saw in Nigeria: *No condition is permanent.* Now, I don't like that statement any more and no longer believe that it is true. The Ratified Evidence About Life has revealed that the statement *'No condition is permanent'* is not true and that it can be misleading actually.

The sun is permanent and it permanently shines. The *condition* or place of the sun in this world is permanent and the *condition* or event of the sun shining is *permanent* also because the sun would always shine even if it does not shine on you because your part of the earth has moved away from it.

Failure is a condition just as success is a condition. Failure is permanent when you don't get real. Conversely, success is permanent when you get real.

The danger presented by the misguided statement that *'no condition is permanent'* is that *you* cannot permanently succeed or continue to succeed in life. The worrying meaning of the statement is that even when *you* succeed in life you MUST then fail because your condition of success cannot be permanent. This is false; and it must be a curse! People who tell you that you cannot succeed and continue to succeed in life must be cursing you. You don't *need* that curse and I am sure you really don't *want* it either!

The Ratified Evidence About Life has revealed a secret: you can succeed in life when you get real and you can permanently continue to succeed in life when you permanently get real; that is, when your position in life, like that of the sun, is permanent. *The position that you must permanently occupy in order to permanently succeed in life is to get real.* When you get real you would definitively shine in life and you would permanently shine as long as you permanently get real.

I would like to use the example of an area of life – marriage – that I am currently working on to further illustrate and support the real point being made in this passage. In a few days' time after writing this passage, I would be providing another marriage seminar in London. There is plenty of evidence to show that some marriages break up or break down just as there is plenty of evidence to show that some marriages permanently succeed. As with all other areas of life, the explanation for the success or failure of marriages lies in whether or not the parties involved get real with their marriage.

My parents had a successful marriage and their marriage was permanent because **they both got real**. They were permanently married for about forty-three years until the death of my father. My wife's parents have been permanently married now for about sixty years and they are still continuing to succeed in their marriage as I write this passage because **they both got real**.

Happiness – a form of internal success – is also a condition. You can permanently be happy by getting real; and you would permanently be sad if you do not get real. Wealth and poverty are conditions also. You can permanently be wealthy by getting real; and you would permanently remain poor if you do not get real.

Overall, you can permanently succeed in life by getting real. On the other hand, if you don't get real, you would permanently fail.

There are definitely some conditions in this real world that can be permanent and success is one of them. By permanently getting real, you definitely can permanently enjoy your journey of success.

The journey of life is truly like riding a bicycle: you fall off or fall down only if you do not *permanently properly pedal*. I call this the *Three Ps* of the journey of life. Like every other point in this book, you can simply sum it up in two simple words: get real.

People who get real in life don't fall down; and like the sun, when they 'go down' – without falling down – they eventually rise and shine again.

Success is a *need*. **A need is a necessity. People often say that 'necessity is the mother of invention'. This is true. But having the need or necessity to succeed is not enough. This explains why everyone does not actually produce or deliver success even though everyone has a** *need* **or a** *necessity* **to succeed.**

Because life is the outcome or product of a biological process, success in life is the outcome or product of a biological process also. Given that necessity is the 'mother' of invention, the Ratified Evidence About Life has shown that a 'mother' alone cannot and would never be successfully productive even in a test tube or elsewhere in our real world without the fertilising enabling agent of a 'father'. Even self-pollinating plants – that have life also – must combine a 'mother' with a 'father' in order to succeed in being productive. This is a hard fact of life.

When we apply the useful and relevant biological description of necessity being the 'mother' of invention to personal success in life, we must have a bonding or combination of both the 'mother' and the 'father' of success in order to deliver or produce our personal success in life.

The Ratified Evidence About Life reveals that although necessity is the 'mother' of invention – including personal successes – getting real is the 'father' of invention. The Ratified Evidence About Life also reveals that success in life originates and is produced ONLY from the fusion of the 'mother' and the 'father' of success.

In order to successfully invent something including succeeding in any area of life, as well as having the necessity for it or the need to succeed in that area, you must also get real. You must fertilise your need to succeed by getting real.

The Ratified Evidence About Life also demonstrates amongst many other things that when people's ways of, and approaches to, life are analysed as this book does, it would be apparent that not everybody wants to succeed; not everybody decides to succeed; and not everybody consciously does things to ensure their personal successes in life.

The hunger for success or the *need* for success is not food for thought. It is a real need; and you must get real in order to fulfil your need for success. When you consciously decide that you want something, you would seek to *do* things that would help you to get what you want. Therefore, in order to succeed in life, you must want to succeed. *Although everyone needs to succeed, only people who want to succeed and then get real actually succeed.*

By deciding to proceed with studying this book, you have demonstrated your desire to succeed. You have shown that you want to succeed. And we are on the same wavelength. I want you to succeed also. This is my reason for writing this book for you.

But I do not take credit for what other people *do* and would not take the credit for your personal success as a result of *your* application of the real secret of success that this book reveals to you. I like what Indira Gandhi, a former Prime Minister of India said:

> *My grandfather once told me that there are two kinds of people; those who do the work and those who take the credit. He told me to try to be in the first group, there was less competition there.*

When *you* succeed as a result of applying the secret that this book reveals to you, *you* and *you* alone are responsible for your own success and *you* should duly take the credit for it. If you fail, *you* and *you* alone are responsible for your own failure.

Nobody and definitely no book can *make* YOU fail or succeed in life just as nobody and definitely no book on cooking can *make* YOU eat food. Nobody *makes* the sun shine. Like the sun, it's really up to each person to shine in this world. In order to shine in life, we must act like the sun: just shine and continue to shine!

Although human beings need to succeed, only human doings lead to success! The point about human *doings* does not mean that you should become a workaholic or stress yourself out in order to succeed in life! Rather, you can and should do what you enjoy and enjoy what you do.

The point about human *doings* does not also mean that you should not relax. Successful people DO relax, they DO have and enjoy a break, they DO make time for themselves and for other people, and they also DO other things associated with success.

Successful living is about getting the right balance in life. Just as being a workaholic is not good for you, being lazy and just having a lie in is not good for you also.

The *London Metro* newspaper recently reported the danger of having a lie-in in an article entitled "*A lie-in could kill, warn scientists*". The article really offered something to people who enjoy having a lie in to sleep on.

The newspaper reported that people who sleep longer than eight hours are more likely to die young than those who sleep for six or seven hours a night. The report was based on research carried out by American scientists who studied one million people over a six-year period.

Whilst the researchers acknowledged that additional studies were needed to determine if setting your alarm clock earlier could actually improve your health, their studies, nonetheless, point to something that should interest everyone: being a workaholic is not good for your health and does not help you to succeed in life, just as being a layabout is also not good for your health and would not help you to succeed in life either!

I provide management training courses for a wide range of people including chief executive officers of large and small organisations, directors, managers, supervisors, junior staff as well as unemployed people on various mentoring schemes and the British Government's *New Deal* programme.

Many unemployed people have reported the shocking way in which they spend something we all have in common: time.

Some unemployed people have reported directly to me on various personal development training courses and counselling sessions that they sleep for up to twelve or thirteen hours everyday, then lie in for an additional three or four hours watching television, and then spend about six hours hanging about with friends or playing computer games that have nothing to do with their job search needs. Given that successful people are not resource-wasters, you would never succeed in life if you waste time, energy, and other resources.

This book challenges you to effectively use the resource that we all have in common – time – as well as your own unique talents to maximise your own personal success in life.

> *It is a disgrace to sleep through the time of harvest.*
> (Proverbs 10: 5)

Only people who have the get-up-and-go to succeed and then *do* things to succeed actually make a difference in their own lives and in the lives of other people.

The evidence presented in this book has been collected over many years and is based on the lives of successful people. The Ratified Evidence About Life contained in this book reveals what successful people *DO* and the evidence challenges you to *DO* things in order to succeed also. Regardless of your background, there is something in this book for you.

Successful people find a way to succeed and they do so only because they have the will to succeed. One of the slogans that I remember reading on a bus in Nigeria when I was a youngster was very interesting: *where there is a will, there is a way*. The statement was written on the bus. The statement reveals a very powerful message. The driver of the bus must have learnt from life that a successful journey is made only when there is a way rather than the mere fact that the bus was on the road. You can hit the road right now but you would not get anywhere unless you find a 'way'. And you would find a way only if you have the will to do so.

Many people who want a university degree know that they need to go down a particular road: engage in university education. Although many people go down that road, only those who find a 'way' to get their degree actually get it. Many people who want to run their own businesses know that they need to go down a particular road: start their own business. Although many people go down that road, only those who find a 'way' actually succeed in owning and running their own businesses. The same principle applies to all other areas of life.

Like the bus previously referred to, other vehicles travel on a road also. But not all vehicles that travel on a road would have a successful journey. Only the drivers who apply the principle written on the bus would have a successful journey: *where there is a will, there is a way*.

A successful journey is made not necessarily because there is a 'road' but because there is a 'way'. Not all roads are passable. When you travel on a road, you might come to a point that is completely impassable. There could be a roadblock, a serious traffic jam, a bridge on the road could have collapsed, or a tree could have fallen across the road. When the road gets blocked, only people who then find a 'way' to proceed with their journey actually succeed in moving forward.

Life is a journey. And success in life is a journey also. There are many 'roadblocks', 'collapsed bridges', 'fallen trees', and other problems on the road to success in life. The road may seem impassable. But there is a secret: the problems or obstacles only block the road to success in life; they do not block *you*! And YOU are the one travelling and YOU would definitely find a way to move forward when you get real!

The fact that all of us are travelling on the road to success in life does not of itself mean that everybody would have a successful journey. Only tough people who are able to find a 'way' move forward on the road to success in life.

Some authors and motivational speakers offer you things like '75 ways' to meet a partner and a different '50 ways' to have a successful relationship when you find a partner; '70 ways' to lose weight; '110 ways' to answer questions at a job interview, and '80 ways' to be a successful Dad or Mom. Laurel Alexander even went further by writing a book entitled *"675 Ways to Develop Yourself and Your People"*.

When you add '600 ways to develop yourself and other people' at work to a different '110 ways' to obtain a job in the first place, to a different '600 ways' to do various things in life – and there are truly various activities in life – you would be required to remember and do many thousands of things in order to succeed in life. This approach is sad.

Most people who hear such speakers or read their books do not even remember six hundred ways let alone sixty thousand ways to succeed in life! And why should they?

You don't need 600 ways to develop yourself at work and a separate sixty thousand ways to do various other things in life. You only need one way: Get real!

The get-real-way works at work and in all other areas of life. The remarkable and successful work of Thomas Edison revealed that 9,999 ways did not work with regard to developing the electric light bulb; only one way did! After trying 9,999 ways, Edison eventually succeeded in finding the one way that enabled him to discover the firmament needed to operate the electric light bulb.

This book makes a very different and fresh statement about success based on the *Ratified Evidence About Life*. What that evidence reveals is that there is a way and only one way to success: Get real. Everybody should be able to remember the one way to success and what the way is: Get real! 'Get real' are two simple but very powerful, empowering and helpful words.

The road to success is there for everyone to use. Rather than take refuge on any of the tempting parking places on the road to success, and rather than lose enthusiasm and then give up when the road seems impassable, you must find yourself a way to move forward in life by just getting real.

'GET REAL' is the signpost that points you in the right and only way to succeed in life. When you get real on the road to success, you would definitely find the way to succeed in life.

Taking to the road to success or commencing your journey of success is induced by your need to succeed but the road to success becomes a way to success only when you construct

and tar it with your personal will to succeed. If you do not have a will to succeed, you are simply on the road and would never find a way to succeed in life. In other words, without a personal will to succeed, you are just leading a wandering life. And what a life that is!

You don't have to lead a wandering life. Just get real and you would find a way to get on! In other words, **get real and succeed.**

3

SUCCESS OR FAILURE IS A MATTER OF CHOICE

*If you think you can do a thing, or think you can't
do a thing, you're right.*
(Henry Ford)

You can if you think you can.
(Norman Vincent Peale)

*I am the master of my fate,
I am the captain of my soul.*
(W. E. Henley)

*… I will not fail, as the others, for in my hands I now hold the
charts which will guide me through perilous waters to shores
which only yesterday seemed but a dream.
Failure no longer will be my payment for struggle.*
(Og Mandino)

*The words YO**u**, S**u**CCESS and FAIL**u**RE cannot be spelt
without 'u'; and 'u' is the only letter that the three words have
in common. You are the only common thing in you, success or
failure. YOU choose whether or not YOU would be a success
or a failure in life. Choose today to take* **'u'** *out of 'failure', and
there would be no such thing as failure in your life!*
(Innocent Izamoje)

I have asked numerous people on my personal development
training courses if success or failure in life is a matter of choice.
Can and do people choose to succeed or fail in life?

Whilst some people answer 'yes' to the question, other people say 'no'. Those who say 'no' to the question normally argue that whilst we do choose to succeed because of the positive benefits and value associated with success, we do not choose to fail because of the cost, pain and loss associated with failure.

People who argue that we only choose to succeed rather than choose to fail actually fail to note that people who do not consciously choose to succeed in life have, indirectly, unconsciously chosen to fail!

People who argue that we do not choose to fail in life suggest that our circumstances rather than ourselves determine whether or not we fail in life. From a hasty glance, this argument seems reasonable; but from a closer examination and on the basis of a more detailed analysis, you would find that the argument that we do not choose to fail is completely unreasonable.

Many different people could be presented with exactly the same circumstances in which all of them **could choose** to succeed; but whilst some of them would get real and choose to succeed by controlling their circumstances, other people would choose not to succeed by letting their circumstances control them. **We are an integral part of our circumstances; and we are the single most important, powerful and controlling part of our circumstances.**

Evidently, like other aspects of life to which we all respond, success or failure in life is a matter of choice. We determine and are responsible for the way in which we respond to situations in life – including success or failure. The word 'responsibility' indicates our 'response-ability'. In other words, we have the ability to respond to situations in the way that we choose. Similarly, the word 'accountability' with regard to living life means our ability to give a good or a bad account of anything we are engaged in. You are your own life-account manager!

I would give you an example of something I noticed at a shopping centre recently to illustrate this point. Two men on a busy street were verbally abused by a passer-by. One of them chose to be upset by what the passer-by said to the two of them and verbally lashed out at the passer-by but the other man chose not to be upset by the passer-by and did not abuse the passer-by back; he did not even make a single comment.

In effect, the circumstance faced by the two men described in the preceding paragraph was exactly the same. However, although they were faced with exactly the same circumstance, their perception, interpretation and response to the same circumstance was different. To put this point differently, they individually *chose* the way in which they perceived, interpreted and responded to the same circumstance.

CHOICE IS OUR COMMON NAME

I once met a woman called Choice. She owned and managed her own small business in Warri – a town in Southern Nigeria.

I remember, on one occasion when my family and I visited Nigeria, Choice came to my sister-in-law's house to buy some items that were on sale. Like the other people who looked through the various items on sale on the day, Choice only chose and then bought the items she was interested in.

Of all those who bought various items on the day, she was the only person called Choice. I remember joking with her by asking her if she had made her choice and chosen exactly the items she wanted. I presented her with some items and then joked by saying *'Choice, please make your choice'*. I told her that I was attracted to her uncommon name – Choice – because most people who meet me tell me that I also have an unusual name – Innocent. In fact, sometimes, I jokingly introduce myself to other people as 'Innocent not guilty', just for a laugh!

But what is not a laughing matter in life is that everyone is called 'Choice'. **Regardless of whatever your own personal name is every person is Choice. In our real world, people are called or referred to by what they DO.** If you drive a car, you are a driver; if you sing, you are a singer; if you sail, you are a sailor; if you teach, you are a teacher; in fact, you are called whatever you DO.

Even if your name is 'Jack' or 'Jill' or 'Adam' or 'Eve' or something else, regardless of our different names we all DO one thing in life: we all make choices. And because we are called what we DO, someone who is engaged in *choosing* is called Choice. This is my reason for asserting that we all have a common name: Choice.

There are things in life regarding which there is only one right choice. For example, choosing to breathe. It cannot be right to choose not to breathe and then kill yourself. If something is wrong, there can never be a right way to do it. To choose to stop breathing is wrong. Similarly, with regard to success or failure in life, there is also only one right choice to make: choose to succeed.

In the journey of life, there is never a right way to go down the wrong road. Failure is going down the wrong road. And I truly mean going down!

We all make choices regardless of whether or not we realise that we make choices in life. With regard to the subject of this book – success – the choices facing us in life are twofold: we consciously choose to succeed or unconsciously choose not to succeed; in other words, we unconsciously choose to fail. Because this book deals with success, it challenges you to a new vision of life – you can succeed in all areas of your life if you consciously choose to succeed.

It makes a very big difference when you consciously choose to do something. I remember the first time that I deliberately and consciously made a choice to be happy within myself. After struggling within myself over many years to be a happy person, I eventually realised that the only difference between happiness and sadness was my own choice and that I could consciously choose to be happy or unconsciously choose to be sad by not consciously and deliberately choosing to be happy.

By making a conscious and deliberate choice and effort to be happy, it was no longer a matter of simply saying to myself that I wanted to be happy. Everybody can say to himself or herself or to anyone else that they want to be happy. In addition to saying things, we must DO things. Not everybody does specific things to promote their *own happiness* or the happiness of other people around them.

Like most people, I had previously only always said to myself that I wanted to be happy without setting sound and specific goals and DOING things to activate or ensure my own happiness. Like most people I simply talked but did not *do*. And like most people, I failed to learn the crucial lesson in an appropriate and meaningful Chinese proverb: *talk doesn't cook rice*!

Like other aspects of success and failure, we choose either to be happy or to be sad. And like other aspects of success and failure, if we do not consciously choose to be happy, then we have subconsciously or unconsciously chosen to be sad.

The first time that I deliberately and consciously made the choice to be happy, I drafted and then signed in the presence of witnesses – my children – a written personal happiness contract with myself. By putting my personal happiness contract in writing, it helped me to focus my mind on the contract and to activate it as contractually agreed with myself.

Since drafting my first personal happiness contract, I have learnt a lot from myself and other people and have refined the original contract in line with the principles set out in this book; and in particular, in line with the principles contained in the section on setting *SMARTER* goals.

My current personal happiness contract contains various examples of sound and specific things that I personally seek and plan to do on a daily, weekly, monthly, and yearly basis. It contains examples of how I would practice forgiveness; seek feedback from myself and from other people; reward, support and help other people and charitable organisations by offering them money and gifts, praising them, and so on; my engagement in voluntary work; and other sound and specific things that I plan to do to promote my own personal happiness and the happiness of other people around me. I would like to specify an example extracted from my own personal happiness contract:

> "Every year, I would use my birthday to fully reflect on this happiness contract with myself and analyse the ways in which I have contributed to my own personal world and the wider world around me. I would spend about an hour on my birthday to write down the main findings of my self-assessment and how, during the preceding year, I have improved my own world and the wider world around me".

With regard to the point about promoting our own personal happiness and the happiness of other people around us, I would like to emphasise that we can promote our own happiness and then personally choose to be happy; but although we can and should promote other people's happiness, it is for other people personally to *choose* to be happy.

You cannot *make* another person happy. People *make* themselves happy. In order to be happy in this world you must deliberately and consciously personally choose to be happy. People rightly or wrongly interpret from their own personal perspective, the way in which they perceive other people as treating them. Even if other people offend you – intentionally or unintentionally – YOU cannot *take* offence if you don't mean to or want to.

Regardless of the way in which you think other people treat you, the fact nevertheless remains that you have the personal power to choose to *make yourself happy* if you want to!

If you act in a malicious, untrustworthy, unfriendly, dodgy or iffy way towards another person, it would be more difficult for the other person to promote your happiness as they would be less motivated or inclined to do so. A crucial component of the strategy for making yourself happy with regard to your relationship with other people is to treat other people in a manner that motivates and encourages them to treat you in a way that assists you to *make yourself happy*.

For reason of space, I have chosen not to reproduce my current four-page personal happiness contract here. In the section following, I would set out a short extract from the written personal happiness contract that I drafted, agreed, and entered into with myself.

☺ *SUCCESSFUL HAPPINESS* ☺ *CONTRACT*

"I, Innocent Izamoje, do solemnly declare and commit to the following principles; namely, that:

- I have rights including my legal rights, … and a natural right to be happy …
- I have a right to choose to exercise my rights or to choose not to exercise my rights. I hereby choose to exercise my natural right to be happy.
- I cannot *always* control every single situation including natural disasters and what other people do – for example, what other people might say or do to upset me – but I can always control MY RESPONSE to what other people say or do to me, or what any situation might present.
- I am consciously and conscientiously entering into this happiness contract with myself because I know that it is in my own self-interest to do so for many reasons … .
- I fully understand and accept that this is a life-long commitment. …"

After drafting and duly considering the contract, I called my two young sons into my study room and read out the contract aloud to them. Before reading out the contract to them, I explained to them what I wanted to do with it. You could imagine how the ceremony felt like. A father personally declaring to be happy and then signing a personal written declaration to this effect in the presence of his children after explaining it to them and then reading it aloud to them!

I asked my sons to assist me by regularly reminding me of the personal happiness contract especially if they had any reason whatsoever to feel or believe that I had breached my own personal happiness contract regardless of whether or not anyone else or myself agrees with their view.

I signed my personal happiness contract in the presence of my young children because, as any parent should know, young children quickly remind you if you do not keep any promises you make to them or if you say one thing and then do a different thing. Adults might overlook it if you do not keep a promise; but young children are more likely to remind you to fulfil your promise! I creatively and constructively used this energy and persuasive influence that young children have so that my children would remind me if and when I breached my own personal happiness contract; and thereby help me to get back on track on the road to successful happiness.

I am grateful to my children for agreeing to work with me and for keeping their side of our 'deal' by regularly reminding me of my personal happiness contract.

I am glad that I chose to construct and sign the personal happiness contract with myself. There is power in choice. We should channel that power into constructive energy by making the right choices in life. You definitely feel good when you do!

Truly, life is about making choices. Choice is not just a name that some people are called. Choice is the only name we all have in common because we all make choices in life.

A valuable gift is truly valuable only if you appreciate and use it. Therefore, value and begin to use the gift offered to you in this book and consciously choose to make failure a thing of the past.

The point about consciously choosing to make failure a thing of the *PAST* is a fundamental aspect of the real secret of success. This point is analysed in the next Chapter that demonstrates that you can succeed only if you consciously choose to succeed and then do things that make failure a thing of the *PAST*.

4

HUMAN DOINGS MAKE FAILURE A THING OF THE *PAST*

Success is simply a matter of luck. Ask any failure.
(Earl Wilson)

The harder I work, the luckier I get.
(James Thurber)

*Success in life does not happen by chance. Even a miracle is activated by DOING; that is, by doing something or a combination of things such as believing, applying faith, praying, working, and so on. If manna were miraculously to fall down from heaven without your intervention, YOU still have to DO something on the planet Earth: catch it.
Success in life is about DOING.*
(Innocent Izamoje)

Talk doesn't cook rice.
(Chinese Proverb)

We enjoy ourselves … in our doing; and our best doing is our best enjoyment.
(Friedrich Jocobi)

Human beings do not create success; only human doings do. *Being* something does not and cannot create or lead to success; but *doing* something can create and lead to success.

When you get real and then succeed, if anyone tells you that you are successful because you were a lucky person, do not argue with him or her. Just get real with them: save your breath! Don't waste your breath or time on people who don't get real in life. Successful people do not waste resources including their breath and time. As Arthur Block reminds us, *"never argue with a fool – people might not know the difference"*.

It is what we DO rather than who we are that is associated with whether or not we would be successful or continue to be successful in life. Being a human being is associated with what we all are or what we all have. We all have biological characteristics, for example, as male or female beings, and we all have a mind, and so on.

What you have would not do anything for you if you do not do anything with it. For example, as human beings, our hands or brains could not and would not produce anything unless we DO something with them. This is my reason for saying that human beings do not create or lead to success and that only human doings do. True.

> *I hear, I forget*
> *I see, I remember*
> *I do, I understand.*
> (Chinese proverb)

The clue to understanding the real secret of success and to succeeding in life is 'DOING'. People who get real are doers and the first thing they do in order to succeed in life is to get real. With regard to success, that is a powerful and refreshing word: DOING! The word 'doing' is the present continuous tense of the word 'do'. 'Doing' implies that we should continuously be doing something to seek, obtain, and then retain success.

The Chinese proverb specified in the preceding section is very appropriate indeed:

> We forget what we hear.
> We remember what we see.
> We understand what we DO.

A crucial part of the real secret of success is:

UNDERSTANDING WHAT YOU DO AND DOING WHAT YOU UNDERSTAND

One of the key characteristics of successful people is that they do what they understand and understand what they do. This contrasts with a lot of people who do what they do not understand and do not understand what they do.

'Doing' can lead to differences between different human beings, as well as differences between a particular person's successes in different areas of his or her own life. The only way to succeed in life is through getting real and then *doing* things that make failure a thing of the *PAST*; that is, through Personally Activating Success Today.

Say this to yourself: *I would make failure a thing of the* **PAST** *by*

Personally
Activating
Success
Today

Repeat the preceding statement to yourself by using your own first name. In my case, because my first name is Innocent, I have just said to myself that '*Innocent is Personally Activating Success Today*'. Put your own first name in the space provided below and quietly but convincingly and persuasively repeat the statement to yourself:

... is Personally Activating Success Today.

You should be enjoying this. Therefore, declare it to yourself again:

... is Personally Activating Success Today.

Well done!

Believe that you are personally activating success today. A crucial aspect of the real secret of success is that **successful people believe what they say and say what they believe.**

In order to achieve success and make failure a thing of the *PAST*, you should note the importance of what each letter of the abbreviation *PAST* represents. In the sections following, I would deal with each letter of the abbreviation *PAST* and the issues associated with them.

PERSONALLY

Success comes in a can ... "I can!"
(Wally Amos)

If you would be well SERVED, serve yourself.
(J.E. Austen-Leigh)

The letter 'P' in the abbreviation PAST stands for the word 'personally'. Successful people personally take responsibility for their own success. In order to become successful and to continue to be successful, you have to personally take responsibility for *your own* success.

You should not and must not give up personal responsibility for your own success in life. If this point sounds like a wake up call, then you'd better wake up right now and personally take responsibility for your own success!

There are some issues regarding which individuals do not have the entire responsibility for ensuring success. If you are in a relationship (for example, a marriage or a business partnership) the parties to the relationship individually – and thereby, jointly – have the responsibility for ensuring that the relationship is successful.

Both parties – in a marriage or other forms of relationship – must do their own bit to ensure the success of the relationship. Arguably, even in circumstances where there is a shared or collective responsibility for success, the fact remains that the responsibility for success is still personal. In other words, *each person* in a relationship *personally* has the responsibility for activating success in the relationship.

By individually personally activating success the parties in a relationship would maximise the benefits of their joint efforts; after all, collective responsibility is the sum of the individual responsibilities of *each* person!

There is a popular saying from where my parents originate in Nigeria that **nobody can look after *your own* for you as well as, let alone better than, *you*. If you think that other people would look after *your own thing* for you better than you personally would, then you'd better get real!**

You must live up to your own responsibility by personally taking charge of your own success. You are personally responsible for your own wake up call in life and for what you do or do not do when you wake up.

When you have accepted your personal responsibility for your own success, the next thing to do – yes, to DO – is to activate success and continue to activate it.

ACTIVATING

Things do not happen. They are made to happen.
(John F. Kennedy)

Talking is not like doing.
(Lebanese Proverb)

Diligence is the mother of good luck.
(W. Stepney)

The letter 'A' in the abbreviation *PAST* stands for 'activating'. The word 'activating' is the present continuous tense of the word 'activate'. Successful people activate success and then keep activating it in order to remain successful. They do not stop seeking to succeed today just because they succeeded 'yesterday'.

Pride or extreme self-satisfaction is dangerous. Successful people are not proud or lazy because they know that proud or lazy people are not successful. Therefore, you must be prepared not just to personally activate success but to continuously personally activate your own success.

You do not have to do anything to attract failure. Failure comes to people 'naturally'. Therefore, the only way to avoid failure and then succeed in life is through intervention. This is a crucial law of nature. If you want to sit for an examination at school and want to fail the examination you simply have to do nothing; in fact you don't even have to bother turning up for the examination. It is that simple. But if you want to succeed you must do something and properly do it.

You don't have to struggle to fail or to attract failure. True. If you do something to attract failure you would get it in abundance!

Unlike failure, success does not just come to you. You have to do something, and more importantly, you have to properly do something to succeed in life. The more you properly do something to activate success, the 'luckier' you would be with regard to being more successful. The relationship between luck and success is simple: you would be lucky to succeed in any area of life only if you activate success and continue to activate success in that area.

Even in circumstances where everything *seems* to be entirely dependent on luck, you still have to *do* something to be lucky. Many lottery winners have reported that they thoroughly thought through the numbers that they selected; for example, that they used dates of birth, house numbers or other combination of numbers. Even if they did not work at the numbers that they chose, they still had to *do* at least one thing: buy a lottery ticket.

I remember a joke we had on one of my personal development training courses where we analysed the issue of doing something in order to activate success. Someone on the training course wished that his chosen lottery numbers would turn up on the following Saturday night lottery draw organised nationally in the United Kingdom. He went on saying what he would like to do with his millions if he won the lottery jackpot.

One of the other participants on the training course asked him to kindly remember her if his chosen numbers turned up and he became a millionaire. The positive thinking participant replied that he would not remember the other training course participant. When the other participant enquired why the positive thinker would not remember her if he won the lottery jackpot, the positive thinking participant replied: '*because you cannot wish for yourself*'.

To dream or wish for *you* personally to succeed in life requires very little or no energy, and it does not require any action at all. Yet, many people do not wish for themselves. Many people just do not *do* things; including doing the simplest of things such as merely wishing for themselves to succeed. The lack of action on the part of many people is the single greatest hurdle to their personal success in life.

Successful people do not believe that a hurdle is something you stumble upon; rather, they see a hurdle as something you jump over, go round or if necessary, go under or even go through! Such actions might involve reasonable risk taking. Successful people take reasonable risks.

SUCCESS

These success encourages: they can because they think they can.
(Virgil)

The letter 'S' in the abbreviation PAST represents 'success'. Success is what you should aim your personal activation at. Focus on it. If you do not focus on success, failure would automatically take its place.

Many people have been known to say things that indicate that they do not know why they fail. Many people say things like: *'why did this happen to me?' 'I can't believe this is happening to me'; 'it's like I'm dreaming!'* And they are dreaming indeed. They need to wake up to reality by getting real.

Most people don't know why they fail because failure comes to people automatically regardless of whether or not they do something to attract it.

On the other hand, people who succeed in life know exactly why they succeed because they focus on and activate success. You never hear successful people say things like *'I don't know why I am successful'*. Successful people know why they succeed in life.

Whatever is done to activate success is a form of work. Successful people work and they work very hard and work very well indeed. They know for sure that:

THE ONLY PLACE YOU FIND SUCCESS BEFORE WORK IS IN THE ENGLISH DICTIONARIES.

With the single exception of the English dictionaries, you would never find 'success' before 'work'. In real life success comes after, not before, work.

People who seek to find success before work in life are merely dreaming and they would keep dreaming forever because they would never find success before work in life. Everybody dreams.

THE CONTINUOUS PROBLEM IN LIFE IS NOT DREAMING. CONTINUOUS DREAMING IS THE PROBLEM IN LIFE.

A key difference between successful people and unsuccessful people is that unsuccessful people keep on dreaming whereas successful people take personal responsibility for their own wake up call in life, and then actually wake up and take the necessary steps required to turn their dreams into reality in life. Successful people know that they are living in a real world not in a dream world somewhere else!

TODAY

Jam tomorrow and jam yesterday, but never jam today.
(L. Carroll)

In my abbreviation *PAST* the letter 'T' represents 'today'. 'Today' is the only day that you have to activate your own success.

Unlike 'today', 'yesterday' has come and gone and would never come back; and unlike 'today', 'tomorrow' would never come. If you leave until 'tomorrow' what you can and should do today, you would have missed a vital aspect of the real secret of success in our real world. Common sense shows that there is no such thing as 'tomorrow'. Honestly.

THE ONLY PLACE WHERE TOMORROW COMES AFTER TODAY IS IN THE ENGLISH DICTIONARIES.

In our real world tomorrow never comes after today because there is no such day as 'tomorrow'.

When I was about eight years old, I visited a corner shop in an area of Nigeria where we lived at the time. There was a notice that was clearly displayed at the shop by the owner of the shop.

The notice, which was written in a very large print, was clearly displayed near the till. The notice contained the following instruction: "*No credit. If you want to buy something on credit, come back tomorrow*".

On the face of it, the notice carried contradictory instructions. It started off by stating that the shop operated a 'no credit' policy; but it then went on to invite shoppers to 'come back tomorrow' if they wanted to buy something on credit.

However, the instructions are definitely not contradictory. **Tomorrow never follows today. Grammatically speaking,** 'tomorrow' means the next day or the day after today. But success in life is not about 'grammar'. It is about DOING.

Tomorrow never follows today, indeed. If you do not fully understand this point, try visiting the shop referred to in the preceding passage, at least, in your imagination.

When you arrive there on a Monday and want to buy something on credit, the shop owner would tell you to come back 'tomorrow' as stated on the notice. You would then go back there on Tuesday, and he would very happily ask you to come back again 'tomorrow'. And you would keep going back there forever and never succeed in buying anything on credit.

Successful people do not procrastinate. They do not spend today regretting about what they would have done 'yesterday'. They just do it today. They do not leave for 'tomorrow' the things that they only have TODAY to do. They *do* things to succeed in life and they do them *today*. **TODAY means:**

**The
Only
Day
Available to
You**

Today is the only day we have and it is also the only day we have control over.

The great French Marshall Lyautey once asked his gardener to plant a tree. The gardener objected that the tree was slow growing and would not reach maturity for 100 years. The Marshall replied, "In that case, there is no time to lose; plant it this afternoon!"
(John F. Kennedy)

Remember! You can make failure a thing of the *PAST*, only by:

**Personally
Activating
Success
Today**

Remember also that *TODAY* is:

> **T**he
> **O**nly
> **D**ay
> **A**vailable to
> **Y**ou

> *Time is a great teacher, but unfortunately it kills all its pupils.*
> (Hector Berlioz)

You don't have all the time in the world. You only have TODAY. Yesterday has come and gone and tomorrow would never come. Make each day a useful and purposeful day.

UNDERSTAND AND APPLY THE *REAL* SECRET OF SUCCESS

Knowledge itself is power.
(Francis Bacon)

The fox knows many things – the hedgehog one **big** *one.*
(Archilochus)

And you shall know the truth,
and the truth shall make you free.
(John 8:32)

A truthful thing that you must know and accept with regard to succeeding in life is that success is about *doing* and that only doers who *get real* succeed in life. In order to conquer failure and be free from the captivity caused by failure, as well as understanding the real secret of success, you must also properly apply it.

The reason why some people succeed in some areas of life and other people do not succeed in the same areas is simple: those who succeed understand and apply the real secret of success to the areas of life in which they succeed.

Similarly, the reason why an individual who succeeds in one area of life does not succeed in another area of life is also simple: people succeed only in areas of life with regard to which they understand and apply the real secret of success. It is exactly for this reason that an individual may succeed in managing a business but fail in politics.

THE REAL SECRET OF SUCCESS HAS TO BE UNDER-STOOD AND PROPERLY APPLIED IN AN AREA OF LIFE IN ORDER FOR A PERSON TO SUCCEED IN THAT AREA.

Understanding and accepting the principle set out in the preceding paragraph is a crucial aspect of understanding and applying the real secret of success. Associated with this principle is understanding the real meaning of the word 'success' in our real world.

WHAT IS SUCCESS?

Define your success! The more you define it,
the easier it is to find.
(Michael Furber)

The truth is that there is nothing noble in being
superior to somebody else. The only real nobility is in
being superior to your former self.
(Whitney Young)

A practical and relevant way to approach the question regarding the real meaning of success is to involve you in carrying out an exercise.

Remember: you hear, you forget; you see, you remember; you do, you understand. Therefore, carry out the following exercise in order to promote your understanding of the real meaning of success.

Exercise: Understanding the real meaning of success.

- Write down in the Table below the names of five people that you personally consider as successful people.
- Then write down what they did or do, and why you consider them to be successful.

Name	Who This Person Was/Is	What This Person Did/Is Doing	Why You Consider This Person As Successful
1.			
2.			
3.			
4.			
5.			

Optional: If appropriate, get other people around you to inde-
pendently do the exercise as well; then compare
notes with them and you would discover amazing
things that would promote your understanding of
the real meaning of success.

Do not despair if you do not have anybody to compare notes
with. You would also discover amazing things that would help
you to understand the real meaning of success even if you did
the exercise only on your own.

The things that you should discover regardless of whether or
not you did the exercise on your own or compared your notes
with other people's comments are set out in the section following.

Normally, most people do not write down their own names
amongst the list of successful people that they personally construct when they carry out the exercise. Perhaps, like most
people, you did not put down your own name as a successful
person also! Just because you did not write down your own
name or the name of other people, it does not mean that you or
the other people whose names you did not write down on your
list are not successful.

People are successful even if they have not won an *Oscar*
***Award* or *Nobel Prize* or are not listed in *Who's Who*, the**
***Guinness Book of World Records*, or even if they have not**
featured in advertisements, appeared on television or radio
programmes, magazines, newspapers, or posters on a corner
shop window!

Most people would not put down their own names amongst the
list of successful people that they draw up for various reasons
including the following reasons: most people just do not see themselves as successful; most people do not like to show off or pub-
licly praise themselves or even if they do, they have been brought
up not to praise themselves in public; most people believe that
they have not 'arrived' yet and that they could do better; most
people, wish to give credit to other successful people; and so on.

Most people are likely to put down the names of successful
people that they see as their own personal role models or 'idols'
rather than the role models or 'idols' of other people.

Most people are likely to identify as successful people only
those people whose beliefs, life style, or work they personally
approve of; or people that they can personally relate to or associate with in some significant way. For example, most people

who are not boxers or who do not like or approve of boxing are not likely to name Muhammad Ali as a successful man even though he is described as 'the greatest' and was voted as the sports personality of the last century. Most people who are not Christians are not likely to name Jesus Christ or Mother Teresa; most people who are not Muslims are not likely to name Muhammad; most people who do not like to 'acquire' wealth would not name multi-millionaires or billionaires as successful people; most people who do not like royalty would not name a queen or a king as successful; and so on.

Some people are likely to write down the names of popular people in their 'own' little world even if such people do not have a celebrity status in the eyes of the wider society.

The responses to the exercise regarding the identification of the real meaning of success normally indicate that success is both internal and external to us. In other words, there are two forms or levels of success: (a) internal or intra-personal or inner or inward success, and (b) external or inter-personal or outer or outward success. It does not really matter which specific phrases are used to refer to the two levels or forms of success.

Inner success refers to things such as good personal health, happiness, love, peace especially in the sense of having peace of mind or inner peace, having fun, self-esteem, self-confidence, enjoyment, and so on. Outer success refers to things such as power, money, fame, house, car, being in a relationship with other people, and so on.

Having a form of external success does not necessarily mean that the person is internally successful and vice versa. Someone may have a job (external success) but if they are not enjoying doing the job, then they do not have inner success. Someone may have money (outward success) but the same person could be the most miserable person in town lacking inner success! Similarly, people may set a goal to get married (outer success) and achieve their goal. However, the fact that people are married (outer success) does not of itself mean that they have a happy marriage; that is, an internally successful marriage rather than a miserable one.

When most people draw up their list of successful people, they do not name people who are the 'number one' people in a chosen area of life. For example, as I write this book, the richest person in the world is an American man. Therefore, as far as money or personal wealth is concerned, that man is 'number one' because he tops the list of the world's richest people. The richest person in the world could be regarded as an outwardly successful person financially. However, not everybody who names a successful person or even a wealthy person is likely to name the richest (number one) person, and a crucial reason for this is that most people know that to be successful, you do not have to be 'number one' in the sense of comparing yourself with other people. **Real success refers to being number one only in your own world rather than in the world at large**.

There are many outwardly successful rich people who are not 'number two', or 'number three' or even 'number three hundred' or 'number three thousand' on the (unhelpful and completely unnecessary) League Table of rich people in the world.

I know from my own personal experience that success is not about outshining or outperforming other people. At school, I was 'number one' (top of my class) at various stages right from primary school to university level. For example, I had the best Advanced 'A' level result in my large class. I was able to go to a university with my Advanced 'A' level results; but so were many other equally successful students even though they were not 'number one' in our class.

When I graduated from the University of Lagos in Nigeria where I studied for my first degree, I won the *"University's Chancellor's prize for the best all-round student in Political Science"* in a large class of about one hundred students. The Head of the Political Science Division at the university described me as being *"head and shoulders above other students in the graduating class"*. Nonetheless, many other equally successful students happily graduated as I did because we were all successful. I have also been 'number one' amongst my peers in various other settings. I am using my own personal example to illustrate this point so that it does not seem as though I am unduly knocking being 'number one' amongst a group of people because I have not been or could never be 'number one' in a group setting.

Success is not and must not be construed as being 'number one' on the basis of any form of comparison with other people. Being 'number one' amongst a group of people in an area of life does not mean that you are the only successful person or even the most successful person in the group!

In explaining the real meaning of success, most people look at it from various angles with regard to specific areas of life. Most people are likely to write down or identify as successful, the names of people they personally regard as successful from the specific perspective that they were personally looking at – politics, sports, religion, community work, charitable work, business, marriage, family, science, career, and so on. Most people would regard someone as successful in a particular area that they are specifically looking at even though the same person could be described as a complete failure in another area of life.

As used in this book, the phrase 'successful people' refers to people who succeed in any or various areas of life and then use their success to improve their own lives and the lives of other people. If you succeed in business but fail in politics, then as far as business is concerned, you are a successful person.

However, I challenge you to seek to succeed in all areas of your life rather than merely seeking to succeed in some areas. Don't even settle for the lion's share! Seek to succeed in all areas of your life.

Most people who construct a list of successful people are not likely to name someone who succeeded but then 'lost it'. In other words, most people know that success is a journey and that to be successful means to continue to succeed. For example, if you were married and then got divorced, most people would not regard you as a success story as far as marriage is concerned; if you were rich but subsequently became broke, most people are not likely to regard you as a success story with regard to personal wealth; or if you were a President who was accused and then removed from office, most people are not likely to regard you as a success story in politics either.

Success is the progressive realization of a worthy goal.
Success ... may also be defined as the pursuit of a worthy ideal.
(Earl Nightingale)

Most people who identify successful people associate success with a sound and worthwhile belief system defined by the real world. Someone who is notorious and associated with various forms of criminal or evil activities might be a household name but real people are not likely to regard them as successful because of the belief system on which they operate. This fact of life in itself shows that to be successful you don't necessarily have to be a household name.

Most people associate success with what successful people do rather than with what or who they are. In other words, if you have money, then the crucial question that arises is what you do with your money; or if you have fame, then the question is what you do with your fame or persuasive influence on other people around you! If you have knowledge, how have you helped the real world with your knowledge?

There are two types of belief systems associated with success: self-based and other-based belief systems. We all have our own individual belief systems as well as our collective belief systems.

Personally, I believed in getting married to only one wife. My father got married to only one wife, but my grandfather personally believed in having several wives, and he was married to seven wives at the same time. On the basis of our different personal belief systems, was my grandfather more successful than my father or I? I hope you would get real and say 'no'!

Similarly, having seven cars or university degrees does not make you any more successful than someone with one car or a university degree.

And having a husband or a wife does not make you any more successful than a single person, just as having one car or a university degree does not make you any more successful than somebody without a car or a university degree.

> *Our business in life is not to get ahead of others, but*
> *to get ahead of ourselves – to break our own records, to*
> *outstrip our yesterday by our today.*
> (Stewart B. Johnson)

To be successful in life, one has to be the best. Being the best does not mean being number one amongst every other person or seeking to be one-up on other people in the sense of likening life to a competitive sport of winner and loser.

Rather, being the best means being the best that you could possibly be by developing and then fully using your own abilities and talents. Everyone can and should be real winners in life by being number one in his or her own world.

If you are a father, you should be the best father you could possibly be; if a mum, be the best mum you could possibly be; if a teacher, be the best teacher you could possibly be; if a student, be the best student you could possibly be; if a cook, be the best ...; if a footballer, be the best ...; if a helper, be the best ... and so on.

Just as success is shaped by our personal belief systems, so it is also associated with the beliefs held in the wider society in which we live. Because of the notion of sound belief systems associated with success, to be successful is not just about achieving a goal or an objective.

Similarly, to be successful is not just about doing something; it is about doing worthwhile things based on a sound belief system. I would further discuss this principle in the section on setting sound and specific goals.

Success is not just self-defined; it is also other-defined, and both aspects of self-and-other-definitions of success go hand in hand in our real world. If you set yourself a self-defined goal to have your own car and then accomplish your so-called 'goal' by stealing someone else's car, real people would not regard you as successful. This crucial point is associated with the *essential* success quality of sticking to moral and legal principles, honesty, and good conduct or behaviour. **In order to truly enjoy successful living you must have and be seen to have an essential quality:** *integrity*.

INTEGRITY

Integrity is a vitally important part of the real secret of success. The lack of integrity largely accounts for why many people do not succeed in life and also why many people who succeed subsequently 'lose it'.

In order to succeed in life, we must thoroughly know and honestly examine ourselves and be willing to analyse our beliefs, goals, talents, strengths and weaknesses and so forth; and then take the action necessary to ensure soundness and wholeness in our lives.

Many people are not honest with themselves and with other people. For example, if you do not honestly admit that you have a weakness in life, you are less likely to seek to do something about it. We must be true to ourselves. Even if the picture of your life that you find when you take a snapshot of your life is ugly, you must be honest with yourself and then take the necessary corrective action to put things right and lead a decent hassle-free and fear-free life. **Truth is a healing pill. It is bitter to take in, but it does well on the inside of us and truly makes us feel good and at peace**.

As well as applying to the way in which we analyse ourselves, integrity also applies to our relationships with other people and the world around us. In order to succeed, remain successful, and continuously enjoy success, you must always ensure that integrity is a crucial part of your way of life.

The lack of integrity has brought down Presidents; led to broken marriages; led to breakdown in relationships, for example, in circumstances where parents abuse their children or where business partners, friends or siblings cheat each other; led to the loss of liberty; led to the loss of jobs; and led even to the loss of life as some people who were unable to cope with the public humiliation caused by their lack of integrity have committed suicide!

Integrity gives us peace of mind, really enriches our lives and ensures that our sleep is untroubled. **As well as promoting success, integrity also helps us to secure and continuously enjoy successful living and avoid moving from grace to disgrace or gain to pain.**

A SECRET OF VARIOUS INTEGRATED PARTS

I know that's a secret, for it's whispered everywhere.
(William Congreve)

Like human beings, the real secret of success has various relevant parts. We all comprise of various parts: our head, arms, legs, heart, lungs, brain, and so on. All organs of the human body are different but integrated together to make the complex whole that we all are.

On their own, each separate part or organ of the body could be described as useless because they would not serve any purpose on their own. If your head is removed from the rest of your body, it cannot perform the function that the head is designed to perform. Our heart, lungs, and other organs of the human body cannot perform their relevant functions *on their own* if they are removed from our body.

Similarly, in order to increase the positive benefits of each part, we have to properly put together and then properly apply the various parts of the real secret of success contained in various sections of this book.

For example, on its own, the practical value of positive thinking is severely limited if all that you do in life were to think positively. You might be an excellent positive thinker and positively think about everything in this world that you would like to become; but if you do not do something to activate becoming what you positively think about becoming, you would only be building castles in the air without putting any solid and right foundations underneath them.

Similarly, you may have faith in your own ability or have faith in anything; but if you do not translate your faith to the practical level of 'doing', your faith is useless. You might have heard a popular saying that faith without works is dead. You must believe this life law because it is true: *faith without works is dead*!

I would take the preceding point a stage further and add that **positive thinking without positive doing is dead**. This is a hard fact of life. Nobody can change this natural law of life because it is imposed on life by nature.

Thinking is good, and doing is good also. But many people do the wrong thing because, although they are doers, they do not positively think through what they do. Just as 'doing' does not really take you forward in the journey of life if it is not linked into the other aspects of the real secret of success, so also would positive thinking not really take you forward in the journey of life if it is not linked into the other aspects of the real secret of success. Although many people think positively, their wonderful ideas remain only in their heads and never get to the real world because they do not 'do' things to succeed.

Just as we have to properly mix together various ingredients to make a lovely cake, in like manner, we also have to properly put together the various components of the real secret of success and then properly apply the secret of success in order to succeed in life.

PLAY BY THE RULE

Every game in this world has its own rules. The rules governing table tennis, football, basketball, lawn tennis, swimming, netball, and so on are all different. Similarly, the rules for living life in an ideal world and in our real world are different. **Life is a real game in which you succeed or fail in various areas depending on whether or not you fulfil one critical success requirement: Getting real**.

Life is the only game that is real because it is the only game that everyone plays even if we all do not realise that we are playing it. **To get real in life is to really understand and properly apply the**:

> Ratified
> Evidence
> About
> Life

And because life is the only game that we play continuously from cradle to grave, we have to continuously get real and continuously properly apply the **Ratified Evidence About Life**. The **Ratified Evidence About Life** reveals the real secret of success in our real world.

According to the Collins English Dictionary and Thesaurus, to ratify is to "affirm, approve, authenticate, authorize, bear out, bind, certify, confirm, consent to, corroborate, endorse, establish, sanction, sign, uphold, validate".

Therefore, the **Ratified Evidence About Life** is the evidence about life that has been affirmed, approved, authenticated, … and validated by life itself.

If you study every human being in this world, you would find that we all have only one thing in common: life. The only thing that we all have in common is the only thing that truly reveals, affirms, approves, authenticates, … and validates why some people fail and others succeed. The only university that truly teaches every person this hard and indisputable fact of life is the university of life.

COMMON GROUND

In a very significant sense, life is the only thing that all human beings have in common. Other than life itself, there is no other thing that all human beings have in common.

If you take each factor that makes people different – sex, age, colour, religion, and so forth – and then classify or put together people to whom the factor applies in a pigeonhole as the world often does, you would find that people who are put in the same box are not really the same. For example, all men are not the same just as all women are not the same. But all human beings are exactly the same only in one sense: we all have life!

The real secret of success is not based on or determined by what makes people different: sex, colour, size, age, height, class or caste, religion, marital status, nationality, educational background, family background, or whatever else is used to describe or categorise people.

One week before writing this passage, my two sons (aged ten years and twelve years respectively at the time) carried out an assignment for *Children's Express*, a London-based organisation. The assignment was to interview Mr Gurbux Singh, the Chairperson of the Commission for Racial Equality in the United Kingdom for a national newspaper.

Before my children left home to carry out the interview, I discussed with them the kinds of issues that they should examine with Mr Singh. The man is Asian; and I know from the work I do that many people of Asian, African, Caribbean, Chinese, and other ethnic minority backgrounds *blame* racism for their lack of success in the United Kingdom. I thought that it would be interesting and useful for my children to discuss with the man at the top of the law enforcement organisation responsible for racial equality in the United Kingdom why it is that some ethnic minority people fail and others succeed in exactly the same environment. When my children returned from interviewing Mr Singh, they reported back to me what I knew already: that *you* rather than racism actually determine your own success or failure.

In a significant sense, people living today are in a qualitatively better situation compared with those who lived very many years ago. Many years ago, there were no such things as equal opportunities and human rights legislation and other programmes that we have today that are designed to tackle discrimination and promote opportunities for people. In the past, people simply got real, tackled various barriers head on and then got on in life. Today, with the range of legislation and other programmes on equal opportunities, it should, arguably, be easier for people who get real to overcome discriminatory barriers and then get on in life.

Similarly, with the improvements in the field of medical science today, it is easier to overcome the limitations imposed on people by various medical conditions.

Simply reply '**Get real and succeed**' if people tell you that because they are women, they cannot succeed in a so-called 'man's world', or that because they are ethnic minorities they cannot succeed in a world where overall power belongs to White people; or that they cannot succeed because of other reasons such as their age, height, class, caste, religion, marital status, nationality, educational background, family background, personal history including things such as depression, or whatever else is used to describe or categorise people.

The point being made in this passage does not deny the fact that some people are depressed or that there is racism, sexism, ageism, or other problems in society. Rather, the point is that, like many other people who have faced the same or worse circumstances, *you* too can overcome various barriers and get on when you get real.

The real secret of success is based on what we all have in common: life. And everyone who has life can succeed if they get real.

6

SUCCESSFUL PEOPLE HAVE THEIR OWN LANGUAGE

We all write poems; it is simply that poets are the ones who write in words.
(John Fowles)

No one is ever capable of swearing properly in any language other than their own.
(Ben Elton)

Birds of the same feathers don't only fly together; they also speak and understand the same 'language'. Similarly, successful people don't only have the same personal qualities and characteristics; they also have their own real language of success.

In order to succeed in understanding the real secret of success in life, and indeed in order to succeed in life, we need to question and reject some popular sayings or metaphors that disempower rather than empower us; and we also need to create our own sayings or our own real metaphors that empower us and help us to move forward in life. Effectively doing this and using a real metaphor in life is strictly associated with effectively understanding and properly applying the real secret of success.

In the sections following I would cite some examples only for reason of space, regarding the kind of language spoken and understood by successful people.

'DOWN AND UP' NOT 'UP AND DOWN'.

In order to be number one in your own world and feel on top of the world, you must first get down-to-earth.
(Innocent Izamoje)

Fall seven times,
stand up eight.
(Japanese Proverb)

A popular saying that I find really disgusting is the statement 'up and down'; as well as the related and equally disgusting saying that 'whatever goes up must come down'. People who believe such mistaken metaphors are people who fail to get real and, in consequence, go up in life and then fall down!

The real language of success in our real world is 'down and up' not 'up and down'. As well as not saying and believing in 'up and down', I also do not believe or say that 'what goes up must come down' because this is not true in the real world of successful people. The so-called 'law' that whatever goes up must come down is a 'law' that successful people happily break only because it is not a real law as far as successful people are concerned.

Successful people know and believe that they can get to the top and remain there. They only fall down if they stop staying on top, and they stop staying on top only if they stop getting real.

The journey of life is like riding a bicycle. We fall off or fall down only if we stop getting real and thereby stop applying the significant *Three Ps* of success: *permanently properly pedalling*.

There are two crucial times when you should seek to be number one in your own world: when you feel like and when you don't feel like. It is always in your own personal self-interest to get real and succeed.
(Innocent Izamoje)

THOSE WHO GO DOWN COME UP

Just as various forces could pull down something, so do various forces push up something! In the journey of life, successful people use and believe in the word 'push'. When successful living is likened to riding a bicycle, to PUSH means to:

Pedal
Until
Something
Happens.

Successful people know that they want something to happen in their lives and that the only way to secure it is to *PUSH*. You too can push yourself to succeed. Even if you are down or depressed, you can and should push yourself up.

Real success is to continue to succeed. To properly ride a bicycle, you do not just push the pedals once or twice and then coast all the way through the rest of your journey. Coasting would not take you very far in the journey of life. You cannot coast to success. People who get real know that they have to *permanently properly pedal* in order to succeed!

EVERYDAY IS CHRISTMAS DAY

When I was growing up as a young child, I was brought up, like many other children, to treat Christmas Day (25th December) as a very special day. As a young child, when I seemed to be merry and excited as young children sometimes do, adults around me often reminded me that *'everyday is not Christmas Day'*.

Sometime ago, one day during the month of July, I was playing a Christmas carol on my CD player. As I listened to the line *'may your day be merry …'*, I decided that my focus must be on the *'day'* as well as on the *'date'*. The date for Christmas is 25th December, but the *day* for Christmas is everyday indeed.

Not long ago, during the month of September, I offered a lift in my car to a family friend of ours. When she got into my car she was surprised that I was playing a Christmas carol on my car cassette player in September and she clearly made her views known to me.

'What? Christmas carol in September?' she asked in a soft and polite but inquisitive tone of voice. *'Yes, I enjoy the music. It's a shame they call it Christmas carol'*, I replied.

Unlike most people who see only one day as Christmas Day, I see everyday as Christmas Day. **The date for Christmas is 25th**

December, but the *day* for Christmas must be everyday. In life everyday is special and worth celebrating.

To celebrate or show your love for yourself and for other people only on one particular date is like showing love only on Valentine's Day; or being a mother or a father respectively only on Mother's or Father's Day.

In Charles Dickens' book – *Christmas Carol* – Scrooge, who did not make merry on Christmas Day, later changed his mind and thoroughly enjoyed celebrating Christmas. Your middle name is Scrooge if you do not celebrate life everyday!

We should do better than Scrooge and *make everyday we live life a successful day worth celebrating*. Success is not about seeking to succeed on just one day or even for a period of time. Success in life is an everyday thing!

I used Christmas as an example in making my point here. If you do not celebrate Christmas for religious or other reasons, then use your own relevant 'special day' for the purpose of the example and turn everyday of your life into a special day because everyday is a special day worth celebrating.

TOO MUCH OF EVERYTHING IS NOT BAD

You may have heard the metaphor that 'too much of everything is bad'. The metaphor itself is bad.

Saying conclusively that 'too much of everything is bad' raises crucial questions. For example, it raises the problem of what is 'too much'. When does something become 'too much'?

Too much of *everything* is not bad. There is no such thing as too much success. Prior to writing this passage, I carried out an interactive exercise with a group of people in order to determine if too much of everything is bad. During the exercise, it took the group only a few minutes to see the weakness of the mistaken metaphor that 'too much of everything is bad'.

All members of the group stated that having too much of the Holy Spirit is definitely not bad. Conversely, they reported that having even a tiny little bit of Evil Spirit in you is definitely bad!

The finding clearly indicates that the real issue in life is not whether or not you have 'too much' of something, but what exactly it is that you have and the use to which you put what you have. This view that was taken by everyone in the group with which I discussed the relevant issues then moved our discussions on to a challenging and sometimes controversial subject: money.

Many people argue that having *too much* money is bad. As with other things, when does money become too much? If you put this simple question to five hundred or more people, you might get five hundred or more different answers that are correct as far as the individuals offering the answers are concerned.

Understandably, it makes sound sense to question the possession of money in the sense that it is bad to obtain money by *all* means.

In life, the end does not justify the means, neither does the means justify the end. Rather, the means and the end must be justified. This point would further be analysed in the section of this book that deals with setting sound and specific goals.

People who say that having too much money is bad argue that the love of money is bad. This assertion is true.

The love of money is bad. But the money of love is not bad. If the love of money is the root of evil, then the money of love is a root of good.

In other words, the money of love together with other ways of showing love is the root of good.

You cannot have *too much* money if you have the *money of love*. As far as real successful people are concerned, the real issue in life is not whether or not you have money, fame, power, knowledge, or other things, but *how* you obtain your money, fame, power, knowledge, or other things, and *the use* to which you put them.

> *I've been rich and I've been poor: rich is better.*
> (Sophie Tucker)

MONEY DOES NOT MAKE THE WORLD GO ROUND: LOVE DOES!

Rich is better than poor; but money is not everything.

The Ratified Evidence About Life has shown that money is one of the purposeful tools or vehicles – but definitely not the only vehicle – for showing love. When I refer to the money *of* love, I am using the word 'love' in a wide sense to mean the various tools or vehicles – including money – for doing good.

When I say the money *of* love, the word 'of' is used to indicate 'origin' or 'association' as in the statement 'the house *of* my sister'. In other words, my comment about the money of love – the money that originates from love or is associated with love – means that love comprises of various aspects including but not limited to money.

As well as helping other people by directly or indirectly giving them money, we should also offer a helping hand to other people in various ways. The fact that you do something to help other people and that you do it from the bottom of your heart is more important than what you do. Mother Teresa put it very well: *We cannot do great things on this earth. We can only do small things with great love.*

'BELIEVING IS SEEING' NOT 'SEEING IS BELIEVING'

Every great discovery I ever made, I gambled that the truth was there, and then I acted on it in faith until I could prove its existence.
(Arthur Compton)

Most people see what is, and never see what can be.
(Albert Einstein)

A popular metaphor that is contrary to the real secret of success is the saying that 'seeing is believing'.

In effect, people who live their lives on the basis of this misguided metaphor are not doers. They are not self-starters. At best, they rely on other people to lead the way and try out new ideas and they then wait to see what happens from what other people do before believing that the things they saw could be done indeed.

'Seeing is believing' is a very self-limiting metaphor and successful people do not live their lives on this misguided basis. Rather, successful people live and work on the basis that *believing is seeing.*

Believing is seeing indeed. Successful people first *believe* in their own abilities and they believe also that they can achieve what they set out to achieve. Having believed that they would achieve their goal, they then *see* or visualise themselves as having achieved it, work at achieving it on the basis of their faith, and eventually achieve it.

I would like to use an example associated with my favourite sport – football – to illustrate how you can promote your own personal success in life. Given that everyone has the ball at their feet – that is, everyone has the opportunity or chance of *doing* something to succeed in life – you must *believe* that you would achieve your goal, visualise or *see* yourself actually achieving it, keep your eye on the ball, start the ball rolling, keep the ball rolling towards your expected goal and you would eventually achieve your goal.

Throw your heart towards your goal and your body would follow.

If you do not **believe** *that you can jump over a hurdle and then visualise yourself actually jumping over it, you might never try to jump over it. Even if you have the capability to jump over a hurdle you must first throw your heart over it in order for your body to follow. Similarly, before you reach your goal on the road to success, your heart must first get there.*
(Innocent Izamoje)

The principle set out in the preceding passage would be further developed when I discuss the faith approach to life.

Successful people do not wait for other people to achieve a goal before setting out to achieve the same goal. They know from the Ratified Evidence About Life that every great accomplishment in this world was once considered impossible. They also know that they can achieve a goal if they *believe* that they can.

Belief is a very powerful self-fulfilling prophecy. There are many examples of people who believed at a very young age that they would become successful adults and achieve 'X' things when they grow up; and they eventually fulfilled their childhood dreams.

What do you personally believe about yourself? In the space provided in the section following, write down two important things you personally believe about yourself:

Exercise: Personal Beliefs.

Personally, I believe that:

1. ....

2. ....

Well done.

Remember: **Believing is seeing! Just believe the preceding statement and you would see the great things that it would lead you to accomplish in life.**

PRACTICE DOES NOT MAKE PERFECT.

Have no fear of perfection – you'll never reach it.
(Salvadore Dali)

In our real world, practice has never made perfect and it would never make perfect, because practice does not make perfect. Perfection implies that someone does not, has not, and would never make mistakes anywhere, anytime, any day, or in any circumstance. This is not true in any chosen subject or area of life.

Successful people make mistakes. In the journey of life, successful people not only make mistakes but they also learn from their own personal mistakes and from the mistakes made by other people.

Successful people learn from other people's mistakes because they know that, like other human beings, they would never live long enough to make every single mistake themselves. They also learn from mistakes because they are not proud people.

MISTAKES GET PEOPLE INTO TROUBLE BUT PRIDE KEEPS THEM THERE.

Successful people who get real are not proud people. They know that they got to where they are in life and could remain there only if they remain humble. **Truly successful people are not pompous**.

As well as being very boastful, arrogant or big-headed, proud people *think* that they know everything. I did not say that they know everything; I said *they* and they alone *think* that they know everything.

Proud people could hardly succeed and continue to succeed in life. Proud people do not learn. Rather than submit themselves to lifelong learning and to learning from themselves and from other people, proud people *JOKE* with life. That is, they:

> Jest
> Over
> Knowing
> Everything

A proud person is a jester or a joker. But life does not joke with proud people; it catches up with them and severely teaches them a lesson in a hard way regardless of whether or not they are willing to learn such a lesson!

I have learnt from my own personal experiences and from the experiences of many other people who have done a particular thing over a long period of time, that merely doing something over a period of time does not of itself make it second nature. On this basis, I have concluded that practice does not make permanent just as it does not make perfect.

In life, we have to PERMANENTLY PROPERLY PRACTICE. As I have stated already, life is like riding a bicycle: you have to *permanently properly pedal*.

The experience of John demonstrates the need to *permanently properly pedal* in order to *continue* to succeed in life. John studied accountancy and qualified as an accountant. Many years after qualifying, he realised that he had to keep 'pedalling' in response to new developments such as computerised accountancy in order to remain successful.

When a job was advertised for an accountant in his field, John applied for the job because he once qualified as an accountant. He was not even invited to an interview. Eventually, John realised that he had fallen off the symbolic 'bicycle' with regard to his professional journey because he stopped pedalling by not continuously developing himself in line with new developments and changes in his field.

Although I have used the relevant example of John's professional career to illustrate the point being made in this passage, the principle of continuing personal development aimed at enabling you continuously to succeed and meet the challenges that you face in life applies to all other areas of life.

PERMANENT PROPER PRACTICE MAKES PERMANENT.

Yes, permanent proper practice makes permanent. This is what I call the significant **Three Ps of success in the journey of life:** *permanently properly pedalling.*

OLD DOGS LEARN NEW TRICKS

A metaphor that I find really disgusting is the saying that '*you can't teach an old dog new tricks*'.

The **R**atified **E**vidence **A**bout **L**ife has shown that both human beings and dogs learn, and that human beings and dogs learn 'new tricks' from cradle to grave. Learning is not a dose of chicken pox that you catch once in a lifetime and it never recurs.

Successful people of all ages learn new tricks from both older and younger people. In order to *permanently properly pedal* you have to permanently or continuously learn. This is a fundamental aspect of the real secret of success and successful people who are not proud people learn from themselves and from other people.

Even organisations and governments emphasise the importance of continuously learning. Today, in the field of management and organisational development there is something referred to as the *'learning organisation'* and many people talk about life long learning.

Change has become the status quo in life. Successful people change. They change what they do, how they do it, when they do it and so on as part of the process of continuous quality improvement. No matter who or what you are in life, you would, like the dinosaur, become extinct if you fail to adapt to change.

Regardless of whether or not you see yourself as an 'old dog', you must be prepared to learn new tricks and permanently properly pedal in the journey of life. One of the new tricks that you must learn in order to succeed and to continue to succeed in life is to have your own real empowering metaphor that is consistent with the real secret of success.

I invite you to do the exercise in the section following and construct your own real language of success. In order to assist you in carrying out the exercise, I will offer you an example. The example should guide you in constructing your own personal language of success.

Exercise: Effectively Using Metaphors

Conventional wisdom: *Metaphors that limit you*	Limitations: *Ways in which the metaphors limit you.*	Change: *Change the metaphor and construct your own language*	Positive benefits: *How your new metaphor empowers and motivates you.*
Example: 'Seeing is believing'.	This metaphor stops me from believing in my own abilities and so on.	Believing is seeing	Self-esteem; self-starter; taking reasonable risks; inventing new things and so on.
1.			
2.			
3.			

In addition to the spaces specified in the preceding Table, you should use the model set out in the Table to construct other new positive metaphors that are consistent with the language of success.

7

MAKE A FRESH START

The Lord gave us two ends – one to sit on and the other to think with. Success depends on which one we use the most.
(Alan Landers)

The fault, dear Brutus, is not in our stars,
But in ourselves, that we are underlings.
(William Shakespeare)

It is really unfair on God for people who fail in life to blame God.

Rather than blame God, yourself, or other people for failing in life, you should simply do one thing: get real and make a fresh start today!

Successful people make a fresh start by developing themselves and their own circumstances. Do not delay. Construct and develop yourself and your own circumstances today by permanently properly applying the Ratified Evidence About Life.

This Chapter would teach you how to use the characteristics of successful babies, successful children and successful adults to make a fresh start through constructing yourself and your own circumstances and destiny.

Pop star and one of the world's most successful musicians Michael Jackson recently suggested that the world should set aside an annual holiday to celebrate children because they are so *cool*; – the trendy word for 'up to the minute', 'elegant', 'sophisticated', 'excellent', and 'superb'.

According to Michael Jackson, *"there's a Mother's Day and there's a Father's Day, but there's no Children's Day"*.

As someone who works with and learns a lot from children personally, I understand why Michael Jackson wants a world-wide celebration of children. Children and babies bring real value to life in many ways including the different things that adults can and should learn from them.

> *... I am this big kid, and now I get to see the world*
> *through the eyes of the really young ones. I learn more*
> *from them than they learn from me.*
> (43 year-old Michael Jackson)

I like the preceding statement by forty-three year-old – sorry, forty-three *year-young* – Michael Jackson. We all have a lot to learn from the really young ones. Rather than only seeing ourselves as 'X years old', we should also see ourselves as 'X years young'.

In our university of life, as well as having something to learn from successful children, I also strongly believe that successful adults have something to learn from successful babies. Just as babies learn from adults, adults should learn from babies also. I call this learning process being 'baby-like'.

BEING 'BABY-LIKE'

I used to wonder how or why most adults stopped doing something that we did naturally as babies and were actually born to do; namely, *continuously and actively seeking what we need until we get it*. This is something that babies do much better than adults and something that I think and strongly believe that all adults can and should learn from babies.

In order to fully understand the real point that I make here about being baby-like you should visualise a baby who is hungry. Do that now: visualise a baby who is hungry – very hungry indeed. What does a very hungry baby do? Have you figured it out?

A baby who is hungry would continuously and actively do something – cry – until he or she gets food. The urge or drive to continuously and actively do something – which in the baby's example is crying – is a natural stimulus. It is instinctive.

GIVE UP GIVING UP

It's a great life if you don't weaken.
(John Buchan)

The best way out is always through.
(Robert Frost)

Babies who are hungry never give up on their need for food!
True.

If you give them something else – a lovely cuddle perhaps, or
put them in a bouncy or rocking chair to keep them quiet –
rather than give them the food they need or DEMAND they
would continue to actively and continuously seek what *they*
need – food – not what you want them to have – the lovely
cuddle or bouncy or rocking chair. A hungry baby would not
just seek food; they would actively and continuously seek it
until *they* get it.

As I have stated already, human beings do not create success
in life; only human *doings* do. Babies are not just human beings;
they are also human doers. Babies *do* something natural to succeed in our real world. Naturally, they understand and apply a
law of nature: *what you need does not just come to you; you have to
actively and continuously seek it until you get it.*

**Babies give up giving up. This is a life law that everyone
must abide by in order to succeed. Babies are tiny but they are
very effective in getting something – such as food – that they
need. They actively and continuously seek what they need
until they get it.**

Anita Roddick, founder of the Body Shop, was right when she
said something very appropriate: *if you ever think you're too small
to be effective, you've never been in bed with a mosquito.*

Everyone should turn their lives into a bed of roses (something
nice and comfortable) by *doing* what small babies do: actively
and continuously seeking what they *need* until they get it.

If a baby is feeling uncomfortable because, for example, they
are wet and *need* changing, they would actively and continuously seek the change that they need until they get it. As a
parent, I know that in circumstances such as the ones described
in this passage, the only way that you have your own peace is
to give your baby peace by giving them what they need.

The natural learning process helps babies to learn a self-fulfilling prophecy in life: to get what they need they continuously and actively do something. When they continuously and actively do something, they eventually succeed in getting what they need; and this, in turn, teaches them that in order to continue to succeed at getting what they need, they need to continuously and actively do something.

Fundamental to success in life is to continuously and actively do what we need to do to succeed. Successful people are baby-like. Like hungry babies who need food, successful people don't quit. Successful people do what babies do: give up giving up!

BABY-LIKE BELIEF SYSTEM

In addition to the point made above, there is another key aspect of the real secret of success that we should all learn from successful babies. This is associated with our belief systems.

I believe that babies who are hungry do not give up doing something to get what they need because they do not *believe* that they would not get the food they need.

As we grow up, we begin to abandon our natural baby-like state where we continuously and actively seek what we need until we get it. **In order to succeed in life, we must 'grow down' and go back to basics by going back to our natural state of not giving up**. Just as we abandoned our natural baby-like state through a learning process, we can and should go back to our natural baby-like state through a learning process also.

BELIEFS TRIGGER OFF ACTION

Given that believing is seeing, your beliefs trigger you off to take action to get or see what you believe. Action leads to the achievement of results. The results that you achieve and see confirm your beliefs.

You would never succeed in life if you do not *believe* that you would succeed. Everyone has an attitude. It is good to have an attitude. Great! But you must have the *right attitude*; an attitude based on the strong belief in yourself that you would succeed in life. Such an attitude releases your enormous creative power including your thinking power and ability and promotes your personal success in life.

Nobody can ever succeed in any area of life if they have a blocked mind and stop their self-controlled creative power from working for them. I would like to illustrate this point by means of an example that I use on some of my management and personal development training seminars.

I ask people the following 'trigger question' that is designed to trigger off a discussion about successful living: '*How can we eliminate prostitution in two months?*'

I invite you to address the question right now: *How can we eliminate prostitution in two months*? What do you think about this question? Consider it for a few moments before reading on.

What was your first impression when you read the question? Did you *believe* that it is possible to eliminate prostitution or did you believe that it is not possible to eliminate prostitution?

Whenever I ask my training course participants the question regarding eliminating prostitution in two months, they normally respond non-verbally with vexed and curious facial expressions together with a strong shaking of their heads that suggest to me they were probably thinking I had completely lost my mind or was living on a different planet.

Although, initially, people don't say a word in response to the question, their actions speak louder than any words they could possibly use to argue against the proposition about eliminating prostitution. When I then invite people to tell me exactly what they think about the question, everybody offers various reasons which they say and believe conclusively demonstrate that we should not even think we could eliminate prostitution.

Rightly or wrongly, people tell me that prostitution is the oldest profession in the world. Additionally, everyone normally tells me that the question of 'how' to eliminate prostitution is absolutely irrelevant because prostitution can never ever be eliminated and various reasons are then offered by everyone to support their opinions.

After allowing people to give me all their reasons as to why they think and believe that prostitution could never ever be eliminated from society, I then ask them to do me a special favour by thinking and believing for just one moment that prostitution could be eliminated. I plead with them to have a different mindset and consider for just one moment that prostitution could be eliminated. I then ask them to generate ideas that might help us in eliminating prostitution.

Remarkably, people come up with wonderful ideas including the following ideas: governments and relevant non-governmental organisations and agencies should continuously carry out extensive campaigns to highlight the dangers of AIDS and other sexually transmitted diseases; job opportunities should be created for everyone and poverty should be properly tackled; medical research should be carried out to find out why some people are prone to prostitution and how they could be helped to give up the habit; social security and welfare systems should be improved; free counselling and advice should be provided to assist people; prostitution should be made a crime and prostitutes as well as those who use their services should be duly punished; we can and should have a go at eliminating prostitution but two months is too short a time in which to do that; multi-agency working with religious organisations, schools, and community groups should be used to effectively inform and educate people; and so on. The list generated by different groups of people is normally much longer than the shortened version presented in this passage.

After allowing people to generate different ideas that might help us to eliminate prostitution, I then tell them the real point about the exercise, namely that *beliefs and our attitude based on our beliefs can stop or increase our creative thinking ability and can determine whether or not we succeed in life*.

When people believe that prostitution can never ever be eliminated, they would not and could never come up with even one small idea as to how to eliminate it. They even attack you for suggesting to them that prostitution could be eliminated. However, when they change their mindset and then *believe* that prostitution could be eliminated, the same people who, minutes earlier, did not think that prostitution could be eliminated let alone seeing even a single way to seek to eliminate it, come up with various wonderful ideas as to how to seek to eliminate prostitution.

The real point here is not whether or not we can or cannot eliminate prostitution. Rather, the real point being made in this passage is that no matter the problem you have to deal with in life and no matter the area of life in which you seek to succeed, you can generate wonderful ideas that would help you to deal with your problems and succeed simply by *believing and then having the right attitude based on your constructive and positive belief* that you would succeed.

Beliefs highly increase your creative thinking ability, set in motion creative ideas that promote success and drive your personal success programme forward.

Remember: **Believing is seeing**! You must believe it first before you can physically see it. Various people first believed that they could manufacture a car, a telephone, solve their personal problems, do 'this or that thing' and so forth, before they physically achieved their results as desired.

If you do not believe that you would succeed at something you would not even try. If you believe that you would succeed you would have a go at it and eventually succeed.

As my exercise on 'eliminating prostitution in two months' shows, in order to succeed in life you don't have to do anything initially other than to simply get real and *believe* that you would succeed. Believing requires no serious effort or use of energy as such. It is a matter of switching your mindset from one channel to another; and you can easily do it just as most people easily but wrongfully switch their mindset from the 'faith channel' to the 'fear channel' with minimal effort.

When you believe that you would succeed, you would automatically effortlessly come up with wonderful and creative ideas to move forward in life. And because your belief would assist you in focusing on success, you would be able to weigh up your ideas, refine and use them and then find a way to move forward.

Many people who once thought that they would not pass a driving test, that their marriage would not succeed, that they would never buy a house or a car or go on holiday to Paris or New York or elsewhere have achieved their goals by changing their belief systems.

As with life itself, there is always a beginning in everything in life. The starting point for succeeding in life is to get real and then *believe* that you will succeed.

In line with my 'eliminating prostitution in two months' exercise, whatever you are seeking to achieve in life might take less or more than two months to achieve; but that is not the real issue.

The real issue is that by believing that you would succeed in life you would be on track to succeed and your creative mind would enable you to set a *SMARTER* goal; an aspect of which includes setting an appropriate and adaptable timescale. My *SMARTER* goal technique would be discussed in a subsequent section of this book as part of my *GROWTH* strategy.

BE A BABY-LIKE ACTIVE LISTENER

According to an ancient Chinese proverb, God gave us two ears and one mouth so that we should listen twice as much as we talk.

Successful people are good and active listeners. They listen to God and can *perceive* or *just know* something including things that come to their mind from 'nowhere'. They also listen to other people and to themselves – the little voice that we all have on the inside of us.

Active listening is an excellent baby-like quality that everyone must develop in order to succeed in life. 'Listening' is different from 'hearing'. Most adults hear you but they do not really *listen* to you. You must have had an experience with at least one person who might hear what you say but does not LISTEN to a single thing you say.

In some instances in life, not listening could be very dangerous indeed. Some people have been known to hear the driver of a moving vehicle toot the horn of the vehicle to alert them of the presence of the moving vehicle; but, although they 'heard' the blowing of the horn, they did not *listen* to it! This is, sometimes, referred to as absent-mindedness! That is the real point: we *listen* with our *minds* through our ears.

There is a story of a man called Nehemiah who led the rebuilding of Jerusalem after other people destroyed the city in a major attack very many years ago. Nehemiah was successful in carrying out the rebuilding work only because he listened to himself. According to the story, during the reconstruction work, Nehemiah was invited by some people to meet with them in a place called Ono. Although the meeting was presented as a friendly consultative meeting, Nehemiah *perceived* that they intended to harm him. He got real, listened to himself and refused to attend the event.

I once watched a video film about William Shakespeare's *Julius Caesar*. On his way to the venue where he was killed, a man spoke to Emperor Caesar about a scroll that he picked up from a pile of rubbish. Caesar heard him, turned and looked at him but did not LISTEN to him. The scroll contained information on the conspiracy to kill Caesar. Caesar could have taken preventative action if he had listened to the man who spoke to him and presented him with the scroll. As set out in the conspiracy plan contained in the scroll, Caesar was eventually killed; and he was killed only because he was a poor and bad *listener*.

There are many Caesars in this world who kill off their own personal success in life by not actively listening to themselves or to other people or to God. On the other hand, there are many people in this world who have saved lives including their own lives and have succeeded in various areas of life just by actively listening.

My father told me that after a terrible road traffic accident in which I was involved in 1982, six people were recorded as 'dead' at the scene of the accident. According to my Dad, a police officer told him that, just as the police officers who dealt with the case and hospital staff were wrapping up the six 'bodies' to be slotted into a mortuary, one officer heard that one of the supposedly dead people yelped in pain; just once! Therefore, they decided to double check if the short and low-pitched cry that was heard by an officer was actually from any of the six 'dead bodies'.

My Dad further told me that when the police and hospital staff thoroughly checked the 'dead bodies' again, they found that one of them was, to use their own words, "just breathing again". Five bodies were then slotted into the mortuary and the one that was "just breathing again" was taken into intensive care for treatment. I was that one!

I was also told that after my soft cry – just once – to live, I went back into a coma and was in a coma for several days. Just imagine what would definitely have happened to me if the active listening officer did not hear my soft cry!

I did not know that I was involved in a road traffic accident let alone knowing what happened immediately afterwards. All I remembered at the time and all that I still remember now and had previously always remembered was that I sat on the passenger seat behind the driver of the vehicle in which I was travelling before we started the journey. That was all I remembered and have ever remembered. There is truly something called amnesia especially after being in a coma. I have been there before! I knew I was involved in a road traffic accident only because other people told me about it.

Although I have done this many times before, I would like to express my thanks once again to the officer who helped me to live and, in consequence, succeed in life after that terrible road traffic accident by simply doing something that everyone must do in order to succeed in life: ACTIVE LISTENING!

I was told that there were several people in the hospital apartment in which the 'dead bodies' were kept after the road traffic accident. Most of them were 'too busy' preparing the six 'dead bodies' to be slotted into a mortuary, but only one officer ACTIVELY LISTENED to the 'bodies'; and thus saved me from being mistakenly slotted into the mortuary with the five dead bodies that were put in the mortuary.

This is the crucial lesson of my story because it is exactly what happens in life: **Most people are just 'too busy' in life to listen to God, to listen to themselves and to listen to other people**. Most people do not assign a quiet time each day or even each week to reflect on things, meditate, and then listen to themselves; most people do not even seek other people's opinions let alone listening to other people; and most people do not seek God's will or opinion through praying let alone listening to God!

Please actively listen to me as I tell you that active listening is crucial to life and to succeeding in life, for I know and believe what I am talking about; and I am talking about what I really know and believe is true and has saved my own life!

Listening is crucial to successful living. Newborn babies are excellent listeners. Regardless of what you say to them, they patiently listen to you and let you finish. They never answer back until when they are about eighteen months old, or even older!

Listening is more important than talking; and this truly explains why God gave us two ears and one mouth so that we can listen twice as much as we talk.

Most people have got it backwards in life. They struggle for a human right to talk and they get a legal freedom of expression. But they ignore and do not exercise their natural right to listen that is freely given to them by the law of nature.

To use a legal terminology, the right to listen is *absolute* rather than *qualified*. I would like to apply the meaning of 'absolute' and 'qualified' rights in line with the European Convention on Human Rights to illustrate this point. Within the meaning of the Convention, an absolute right is a right that you have that nobody including a government should interfere with; for example your right to life. A qualified right is a right that can be interfered with if there is a legally justifiable reason for interfering in the exercise of the right; for example, freedom of expression.

It should be apparent to you that you have an *absolute right to listen*. Nobody and no government can change a law of nature. This is why nobody can do anything to stop the sun shining. Nobody – other than *you* of course – can interfere with your natural absolute right to listen. Even if other people interfere with your ears in any way, you could still listen to God, listen to yourself, and listen to other people through your mind. This is a simple but powerful and unchangeable law of life. People who understand this life law and exercise their natural absolute right to listen promote their own personal success in life.

By listening to God, listening to yourself, and listening to other people, you might learn new things, receive valuable advice, obtain feedback on your own actions or inactions in life, seek qualitatively to improve your own life, perceive of an idea for a project or for something that could make a difference in your life and in the lives of other people, and so on. Active listening has numerous other advantages.

Listening is like planting a seed. Through listening, *you* plant a small thing on the inside of you and it definitely would grow into something much bigger when you get real and nourish it.

HAVE A BABY-LIKE MIND OF GOLD

Babies have a mind of gold! Take an interesting example: forgiveness. Babies do forgive. For example, whether or not you shout at them, babies just forgive you and get on with life. They still smile at you even if personally you do not smile at yourself.

Most adults do not forgive themselves and other people. I have heard some adults refer to other people as mad simply because the other people practice forgiveness. And yet, when you don't forgive yourself and other people, YOU fill up your own mind with negative and useless business that detracts YOU from succeeding in the real business of life.

It can be good to be mad. Successful people are mad people because, like babies, they do mad or unusual things including forgiving themselves and other people. Successful people are mad about success. And they pursue their vision like mad. Mad does not equal bad.

A friend of mine recently told me that he used to get upset with his wife and also with himself whenever he and his wife had a misunderstanding with each other. He further informed me that when he practiced forgiveness, he noticed the qualitative difference that forgiveness brought to his own life and to his home.

People often say there is no place like home. True. A home without happiness and joy is only a house. Unfortunately, many people live in a house rather than in a home. If you live in a house you must move right now. I challenge you to move from a house into a home on the same property after carrying out a major work: reconstruct and change your mind rather than your property.

A home is built in your mind rather than on land. Getting real, rather than bricks, is the foundation for building a successful home. If people who are living together don't get real, their relationship would break down and definitely collapse like a ton of bricks.

Wherever possible you should let other people know that you have personally forgiven them if they or you do something to upset *you*. Sometimes, however, it might not be possible to communicate to other people that you have forgiven them.

If someone abuses you on the road and then drives off or if someone abuses you at a train station and then catches another train and you do not ever see them again, you can still forgive them. What really matters is that *you* know that you have forgiven them because in a very serious sense, forgiveness is for *you* rather than for them.

In some cases, other people might not even know that they have offended you. Some people take offence just by looking at the way in which other people walk or dress or talk. Even if other people mean to offend you, *you* cannot take offence if you do not mean to! *You* personally benefit from forgiving other people more than they benefit from your act of forgiveness.

You cannot be creative and successfully travel in the proper direction that you wish to go in life if your steering wheel –

your mind – is turned to a different direction. We drive ourselves forward in life through our minds. Forgiveness helps you
to gain your mind rather than to lose it! To succeed indeed, we
must be baby-like and avoid clogging up our minds with things
that do not help us to succeed in life.

**Being baby-like is not the same thing as being babyish, just
as being childlike is not the same thing as being childish.
Successful adults are baby-like and childlike people.**

BABY TALK

As part of the process of recreating yourself and having the
baby-like discipline of *doing*, I would ask you to do one other
thing that babies do very effectively: talk to yourself.

When you talk to yourself, the people sitting or standing next
to you do not have to hear you. Asking you to talk to yourself is
asking you to do a mad or unusual thing. **In order to succeed in
getting an unusual result in life you must do an unusual
thing.** Many successful inventors have changed systems and
practices in various parts of the world and invented new things
only because they were deviant innovators who did mad or
unusual things. You would also find it helpful to listen to people
who have mad ideas.

Take the story of John. He once told me that when his wife initially suggested that they should buy the property they currently live in, he asked her if she was mad. He reported that he
thought she was mad because at the time that his wife made the
suggestion he thought they could not afford to buy a flat let
alone the house his wife suggested they should buy.

However, according to John, after a while, he got real with
himself and with his wife and, in consequence, they sat down
and thoroughly thought through her mad idea together, analysed their own reality, took into account the changes in their
reality, and so on; and eventually, they were not only able to buy
the house but they were also able to pay off the mortgage on
their house within a shorter period of time compared with the
time that they previously agreed with the mortgage lenders.
Today, John is really enjoying the property like mad!

It is unusual for adults to talk to themselves. But this is what
I am asking you to do right now in your own interest. When you
talk to yourself, other people don't even have to hear you. You

should quietly mumble things to yourself as babies do. However, if you are alone, then you can talk aloud to yourself.

Now, get real and carry out the exercise in the section following.

Exercise: Self-talk or Baby-talk

Say to yourself that, like a hungry baby, you would actively and continuously *want* what you *need* until you get it. Believe yourself as you say it to yourself in a solemn but reassuring tone of voice. Put your own name in the space provided in the sentence below and repeat the statement to yourself.

… would actively and continuously seek what I need until I get it.

And again:

… would actively and continuously seek what I need until I get it.

Well done!

Engaging in self-talk or baby-talk is affirming something to yourself. **Successful people effectively use affirmations and talk to themselves**.

ONE DAY AT A TIME

Live life today as though it is the only day you have to live; for it is!
(Innocent Izamoje)

*In trouble to be troubled
Is to have your trouble doubled.*
(Daniel Defoe)

*What's the use of worrying?
It never was worthwhile,
So, pack up your troubles in your old kit-bag,
And smile, smile, smile.*
(George Asaf)

Babies smile, smile smile; they don't frown, frown, frown!

I once listened to a song that stated *'Don't worry, be happy'*. That is an excellent statement: *'Don't worry, be happy'*.

Babies and children, especially very young children do not worry about things. They take and live each day as it comes.

Like babies and very young children we should all live life each day as though it is the only day in which we have to live; for it is! As I demonstrated in the section on making failure a thing of the *PAST*, the only day we have control over is today and TODAY means:

The
Only
Day
Available to
You

In order to succeed in life we must abide by a crucial law of life that babies and very young children comply with: not to worry about 'yesterday' because it has come and gone and not to worry about 'tomorrow' because it would never come. TODAY is the only day available to us to do what is necessary for us to succeed in life and it is also the only day we have to enjoy the fruits of our success.

As well as postponing what they need to do to succeed in life, many people also postpone their happiness. Many people say things like *'suffer before pleasure'* and then live life today – the only day they have – suffering with the mistaken expectation of having pleasure 'tomorrow'. And of course, they never have pleasure tomorrow because there is no such thing as tomorrow! You don't need to *suffer* or lead a painful life in order to enjoy the gains of successful living.

Some people also say *'business before pleasure'*. This is also mistaken because business *is* pleasure. If you do what you enjoy you truly would enjoy what you do. People who do what they enjoy and enjoy what they do, do not see their activities as painful; rather, they see them as fun activities. The work and the gain are one and the same thing.

I really liked something that I learnt from a former work colleague of mine. He told me he never worries about any problem and that we must never worry about any problem in life for two reasons.

According to him, regardless of the problem that you are facing in life, there would be either of two things about the problem: It's either that something can be done about the problem in which case we should not worry about the problem but do the thing or things that could be done about it; or nothing can be done about the problem in which case we should not worry about the problem because nothing can be done about it.

Personally, I believe that even if we think that there is nothing we can do about a problem because the problem is out of our control, there is always one thing we can do about any problem: pray about it. **Even when circumstances evidently are beyond our control in life – such as whether or not it should start or stop raining – we can still DO something: pray about them**! Many people have reported that their impossible problems were resolved by means of this form of intervention – praying.

It follows therefore, that there is no justification to worry about anything in life. It also follows that we should do a baby-like or childlike thing: '*Don't worry, be happy*'. There is no justifiable option and we must do only one thing about worrying: not to do it.

EVERYONE IS A MANUFACTURER

Everyone is an efficient manufacturer. However, rather than manufacture the best things for themselves most people manufacture the worst things for themselves.

People have always manufactured things and continue to manufacture various things in life. There are things people manufacture together with other people and there are also things we individually manufacture on our own.

Personally, for a long time in my life, I have been the only manufacturer of my own personal worries. Like most people, I have personally manufactured worries and anxieties. In this regard, I was truly a very efficient manufacturer and my production line was always very busy.

I used to worry a lot even where I had no reason to worry about anything. For example, at school, although I always had a good grade and topped my various classes on various occasions, I was always worrying and feeling very anxious about sitting for examinations. Rather than see an examination as another opportunity for me to excel, I would worry before taking the examination. In the end, I would sit for the examination and be top of the class. Then the next examination would come and I would worry again about sitting for it. Truly, my ability to manufacture worries was sad and terrible!

As I write this passage, I can now laugh about my old self. But when I was in that state, it was not a laughing matter at all. I am sure you too must have manufactured worries at least once or twice; and if you get real you would recall how it felt being in such a state.

You would see and hear what I am talking about if you watch and listen to the television set on the inside of you right now.

Everyone has a 'television set' on the inside of him or her. Whether or not we realise it, we all have a television set inside us. This television set is automatically switched on when we are awake. When we are asleep, it goes into stand-by mode. The television set on the inside of each of us contains a number of channels that we consciously and unconsciously tune into whenever we are awake.

Just as our visible and physical television sets are named after their own manufacturers, I have also named the television set on the inside of each of us after its manufacturer. I call the television set inside us the MIND TV.

There are significant similarities as well as significant differences between our visible and physical television sets and our MIND TV.

Both television sets come in different sizes and shapes. Just as you can purchase a small or big screen physical television set, so you can also create a small or big picture of success or failure on your MIND TV; and just as buttons or a remote control could control your physical television set, your MIND TV could also be controlled by remotely using affirmations or baby-talk.

Both television sets could be damaged by improperly using the control mechanisms. Just as you could damage your physical television set by improperly using the control mechanisms, so you can also damage your mind by improperly using wrong affirmations or baby-talk.

You would be considerably influenced by what you see and hear on both television sets because they can motivate you or depress you; guide you to succeed or fail; influence your beliefs and opinions; and change your life for better or for worse.

However, unlike the visible and physical television set, our MIND TV is not visible and physical. Other people around you may notice the channel you have tuned into on your physical television set but nobody, other than you, knows the channel your

MIND TV is tuned into. Other people can change the channel on your physical television set without your consent; but nobody can change the channel on your MIND TV without your consent. Most significantly, whereas you and other people can control a physical television set, you and you alone can and do control your own MIND TV.

Your MIND TV has a more powerful and persuasive influence over your life than a physical television set. For this reason, we should tune into the right channel on our MIND TV. Regrettably, most people do not consciously decide to watch and or listen to the right and appropriate channel on their MIND TV.

Although we all have our own personal MIND TV and choose the channels we tune into, a key difference between successful people and unsuccessful people is that, unlike unsuccessful people, successful people tune into channels that help them to move forward in life.

On their MIND TV, successful people visualise and see a picture of themselves succeeding in whatever they are doing; they see themselves enjoying the benefits of their success, for example, they see themselves living in a house they hope to actually move into in two years' time and visualise how they would arrange the rooms and furniture; they hear themselves saying things about their success; they see and hear other successful people and learn from their experiences; and so on.

We all can and should use affirmations or baby-talk to remotely control our MIND TV. Personally, whenever I, mistakenly, tune into the wrong channel on my MIND TV and then see or hear what I don't like, I immediately use my remote control – baby-talk or affirmations – to change the channel.

Honestly, sometimes, before making this change, I might have, unintentionally, watched or listened to the wrong channel on my MIND TV for a few seconds or minutes before consciously using my 'remote control' to change the channel. Everyone's mind drifts. And everyone has the ability to use their own 'remote control' – activated by the mind – to change the channel on their MIND TV. Just as your physical remote control would not change the channel on your physical television set unless you activate it, so also would your mental 'remote control' not change the channel on your MIND TV unless you activate it.

AFFIRMATIONS OR SELF-TALK

My personal affirmations are set out in the section following. My affirmations are linked to the three aspects of our lives: *spirit, soul* and *body*. At the 'spirit' level, I believe that '*If God says yes, nobody can say no!*' At the level of my soul, I believe that '*It is well*' with my soul. At the 'body' or practical level, I '*Get real!*'

- *If God says yes, nobody can say no!*

Many years ago, I placed a sticker visibly on our front door containing the following statement: *If God says yes, nobody can say no!*

Many people who have knocked at our front door such as visitors and post or deliverymen and women have told me they like the sticker. You can't miss it on our front door. It is right there in the middle of the door near our postal letterbox. The sticker fulfils its purpose: it gives me the right spirit. Every time I leave home I have to lock our front door and every time I return home I must unlock the front door to get in and *each time* I see the sticker on our front door it reminds me that if God says yes nobody including me can say no!

I find the affirmation '*If God says yes, nobody can say no!*' extremely powerful because it helps me to manage situations especially situations that are evidently beyond my control. If things that are beyond my personal control happen to me, I simply remind myself that if *God says yes, nobody can say no!*

In order for you to succeed in life and stop worrying about things over which you have no control you must accept the law of life that *if God says yes, nobody can say no.*

No person in this world has control over whether or not it would rain today; nobody has control over whether or not there would be flood or an earthquake today; nobody has control over whether or not there would be 'this or that' other natural disaster in this world; nobody has control over whether or not their loved ones would die; and so on.

Although you do not have control over certain things in life, you can still do something about them; pray about them whilst recognising and saying 'yes' to the law of life that if God permits or allows something to happen, or *if God says yes, nobody can say no!*

By simply saying 'yes' to an act of God you would be doing yourself a huge favour: you would get real, accept life as it is and work to the unchangeable laws of life. Additionally, you would stop seeing yourself as a victim and would stop asking unhelpful questions that do not require an answer; such as '*Why did this happen to me?*'

Victims lose control and personal power and therefore are unable to move forward. Those who move forward in life are people who exercise control and personal power. By saying 'yes' to situations in life in line with whenever God says yes to those situations, you would automatically be able to exercise your godlike power of the mind to remain in control and not to see yourself as a victim.

When you get real you would understand and accept that there are certain things that are bound to happen in life regarding which nobody has control. You would then be able to say 'yes' to the things that happen regardless of whether or not they positively or adversely affect you. And by saying 'yes', you empower yourself and feel in control. You would stop seeing and treating yourself as a victim.

As well as obvious natural disasters there are also 'human disasters' that are intentionally and unintentionally caused by other human beings about which you have no control. As with unavoidable natural occurrences, you must also say 'yes' to unavoidable 'human occurrences' and then move on in life.

For example, you do not have control over whether or not someone else would let you down in life. Therefore, when someone else (including people that you dearly love) let you down in life in any way, rather than become a disempowered victim you should simply get real and say 'yes' that things such as let downs and disappointments are bound to happen in life given that some human beings are a bit or a lot iffy and behave in funny ways.

Playing the role of a victim suggests you wrongfully and unrealistically believe you are immune to being let down or disappointed in this world. Getting real and saying 'yes' to 'human occurrences' would make you see such things as a challenge. You would then be able to make your own decisions regarding how you would respond to the situations and move forward in life.

Although you do not have control over natural occurrences and the forms of human occurrences referred to in this passage, you have full control over *how you choose to respond* to them.

Getting real and saying 'yes' to things that happen in life would enable you to feel in control. You would be empowered to decide how to handle situations and move forward.

Saying 'yes' to unavoidable situations in life does not in any way mean or imply that it is right or O.K. for things that adversely affect you in life to happen; rather, saying 'yes' means that YOU have gotten real and accepted that yes, there are strange, funny, and adverse things that happen to people in life and that you can cope with them rather than escape from life.

The word 'yes' does not only mean 'all right' or 'very well'; it also means 'of course', 'certainly', 'needless to say' and so on. Needless to say there are things that would certainly happen in life that might please you or displease you; but you can choose how you personally respond to or handle the situations by recognising and accepting that, of course, they are bound to happen in life; and in consequence, we should be prepared to properly and effectively handle them.

- *It is well*.

If you use a powerful affirmation or baby-talk to provide an anchor for your personal success programme, it would encourage you to move forward in life. I like another affirmation that I use: *It is well*.

Even if you seem to be going through a difficult time as all human beings do, simply believe that *it is well* and it would be well with your soul even if it were not well with the situation that you are in. There are many people who feel at peace in a bad situation. You may have a disability or you may have 'this or that' condition or situation to cope with or deal with in life and even if your condition or situation is bad, just believe that *it is well* and it would definitely be well with your soul.

Of all living things in this world, human beings are the only ones with the godlike power to determine their own success in life and control their own destinies. Human beings are the only living creatures on planet Earth with the godlike power of the mind; and we are the only creatures that can use our minds to determine whether or not we succeed or fail in life. You would succeed in life only if *it is well* with your soul.

- *Get real*!

I love this affirmation also: *Get real*. Successful people do!

As you can tell from studying this book, I use this affirmation very often and it serves its vital practical purpose: it helps me to get real and remind other people to get real also.

WORD POWER

Words have great power. People can tell you things that could within a matter of seconds or minutes generate great sadness or joy in you. Similarly, you can affirm things to yourself to achieve the result you desire.

Affirmations take different forms. You can repeat a statement to yourself; you can repeat a reassuring word or phrase to yourself in the form of a meditation; you can say an affirmation in the form of a prayer to God; and you can affirm things in the form of a song.

The use of affirmations was the single most important thing that helped me to cope with the tragic and untimely death of my dearly beloved father. I was able to cope with his loss only when I finally realised and accepted that if God had said yes to him living after a prolonged illness, he definitely would not have died when he did. He had been ill on previous occasions and I believed that he survived his previous illnesses and other problems (including being held by soldiers during the civil war in Nigeria) and then lived afterwards because God said 'yes' to him surviving on those previous occasions. **You can cope with what you can't change.**

When I was going through the grief of having lost my father, the recognition of the fact that if God says yes, nobody can say no enabled my *spirit* to connect with my *soul* and it became well with my soul; and this in turn enabled my soul to connect with my *body* and this enabled me to get real and move forward.

When I got real, I accepted, said 'yes' to, and was then able to live with, the facts of life that death is an integral and unavoidable aspect of life and that life and death were beyond my control; but coping with life and death was within my control.

CONTROL MECHANISM

When my mind drifts into the wrong channel on my MIND TV, or whenever I want to personally empower myself, I get real by using any of my affirmations.

I know the importance of word power. It is for this reason that I deliberately crossed out the word 'impossible' in my dictionary. This action reminds me I once believed and should reaffirm my belief that every great thing that has been successfully accomplished in this world by various successful people was once considered impossible.

As well as getting real by effectively using word power through affirmations, successful people also do other unusual things to obtain unusual results in life. I have learnt and applied this principle to my own personal success programme. For example, I placed a mustard seed that serves a crucial purpose for me on the wall in my study where I have pictures of my family and I.

I used a transparent cello tape to stick a mustard seed on the wall in my study room. This small mustard seed performs a very big function for me: it reminds me that even if the faith I have in myself with regard to succeeding in life is as small as a mustard seed, I can achieve what I set out to achieve. And in order to convince myself that my belief in myself is not misplaced or mistaken, I actually regularly look at the mustard seed on the wall and then reflect on various things that I have achieved in life. And this in turn really helps me to get real.

What I am saying in this passage is not unique to me. All successful people do unusual things to achieve unusual results and to drive themselves forward on the road to success.

Keep repeating your appropriate affirmations to yourself until you see and hear on your MIND TV the exact channel you are happy with. Just as you use your physical remote control to continuously change the channels on your physical television set until you see or hear the channel you are happy with, you should also keep using your appropriate affirmations or babytalk to change the channel on your MIND TV until you hear and see the desired channel.

FROM YOU TO YOU

A crucial point about self-talk is to talk personally to your real self.

Affirmations are like a toothbrush: everyone should have his or her own. Even if you have the same brand of toothbrush as the other person next to you, everyone has his or her own toothbrush.

Similarly, even if your affirmations are exactly the same as those of other people or mine, you must personally *own* your affirmations. They must be yours. Affirmations must be personal to *you* and you must personally use them for *you*. You must use your affirmations from your heart. You must say them only because you mean them.

When you ask most people the salutary question '*How are you?*' they affirm '*I'm fine, thank you*' in a singsong manner that does not come from their heart.

Affirmations are not singsong statements. They are statements that connect with your real self. They are testimonials that are deeply placed in your heart and truly reveal the conscious and unconscious desires of your soul.

Exercise: Affirmations or Baby-talk.

Write down the affirmations that you personally think help you or would help you to succeed in life.

1. ....

2. ....

3. ....

Think about and remind yourself of circumstances in which you have previously used affirmations and the ways in which they empowered you. If you have not previously used affirmations, do not despair; there is always a beginning in everything. Just think about how the affirmations would empower you. You would see the ways in which your affirmations would empower you if you look for the ways on your MIND TV.

There are some crucial rules that you must bear in mind when you construct your own affirmations. These rules are set out in the section following.

DO NOT USE NEGATIVE OR MISGUIDED AFFIRMATIONS.

• Avoid affirmations such as 'time works wonders' for time doesn't, *you* do; or 'tomorrow is another day' for it's not! Also avoid saying to yourself things like 'I'm no good' for you would be!

USE ACTIVE RATHER THAN PASSIVE VOICE.

- Say things like 'I am in-charge'; not 'My situations no longer control me'.

FOCUS ON TODAY, THE HERE AND NOW.

- Your affirmations must apply to the situation you are in or are dealing with right now. It is best to construct your affirmations in the form of a present tense or present continuous tense, not future or past tense. I would like to use my affirmations to illustrate this point: '... *God says* ...' not '... God said' or '... God will say'; '*It is well*' not 'It was well' or 'It will be well'; '*Get real*' not 'I will get real'. Remember: yesterday has come and gone and would never come back and there is no such day as tomorrow. Remember also that TODAY means *The Only Day Available to You*. Therefore, your affirmations should deal with today and make you feel in control of the situation that you are dealing with today.

PERSONAL.

- Your affirmation is like your own toothbrush; it must be personal to you. You must own it and say it from your heart.

WHOLE AND COMPLETE APPROACH.

- You comprise of your spirit, your soul and your body. Therefore, you must apply a full approach to the construction of your affirmations and have affirmations that connect your spirit, soul and body together. Even if you use only one affirmation it must enable your spirit, soul and body to connect with each other. For example, when I say 'Get real' and then do, I automatically connect with my spirit and realise that even if I do not have any control over a situation, for example, whether or not it would rain today, *If God says yes* ..., then that is it! In turn, this makes it well with my soul and helps me to stop aggravating myself about a situation over which I have no control.

FLEXIBILITY.

- You can commence using your affirmation from any part of you – your spirit, soul or body. Regardless of the part of you from which you begin your affirmations, you must end up at the 'body' part of you and translate your affirmation into practice.

Given that words are greatly powerful, you must translate your words into action in order for your words to have the desired effect.

As I have stated already, regardless of the part of you – spirit, soul and body – that your affirmations originate from, what is crucial is where your affirmations end up and are given effect. To have the desired effect, your affirmations must be usable at the practical 'body' level.

If, from your spirit level, you say that *'If God says yes…'* you must then end up DOING things at the practical 'body' level that shows that you accept whatever the outcome of a situation is; for example, you do not have to have sleepless nights about the situation. If you commence an affirmation at the level of your soul, you must still end up DOING something that demonstrates practically that *it is well* with your soul. Similarly, if you start an affirmation at the level of the body and say to yourself to *'Get real'* then you must get real!

Having written down your affirmations, the next stage is to commit them to memory. I have used different methods to commit things to memory and you should use any or all of the following methods because they really work:

- Repeatedly say your affirmations to yourself until they become second nature to you.
- Record your affirmations on a cassette tape or CD and repeatedly play back the tape or CD to yourself.
- Write down your affirmations and repeatedly read them aloud to yourself and you would find that within a short period of time, you would become unconsciously competent at saying your affirmations.

I learnt something very interesting from my son, Chidi. He recently told me that he has an affirmation on his mobile telephone. Whenever he switches on his mobile telephone the 'Welcome Message' on the screen states: *If God says yes ….*

That was really interesting. I applauded Chidi for his great idea and requested him to put a similar message for me on my own mobile telephone. Now, each time I switch on my mobile telephone – and I switch it on everyday – I receive the following Welcome Message: *Get real! It is well. If God says yes, ...* Because of the limitation imposed by the settings mechanism on the mobile telephone system, it was not possible for me to write the last part of my affirmations in full. But I know exactly what it says: *Get real! It is well. If God says yes, nobody can say no.*

This is a very interesting way of affirming your belief to yourself and I would like to thank Chidi again for teaching me this method. I recommend it to you also. Truly, successful adults learn from successful babies, successful children and other successful adults.

Additionally, affirmations can and should also be used as text messages on your personal computer screen saver. I have also found this method to be a good way of reminding myself of my affirmations.

Remember: We must do things that are consistent with our affirmations in order for them to work for us.

As well as using affirmations in the form of phrases like many other people, I also use affirmations in the form of songs. When my MIND TV tunes into a channel that I don't want, I sometimes use affirmations in the form of a song to change the channel. If I am able to gain access to my musical equipment, for example, if I am at home or in my car, I immediately play back an interesting song on my cassette player or CD player and then sing along. I recall that my father used to do this. Sometimes, in his study, he would dance to some interesting music on his own.

Most people would agree that singing and dancing on one's own especially where there is actually no social occasion to warrant it – as if you needed one – is a very baby-like or childlike thing to do. But successful people do baby-like and childlike things!

YOUR NEEDS

Most human beings are also different from our symbolic hungry baby in another significant respect: A hungry and crying baby would be satisfied and stop crying only when they get what *they* need – food; not what you think they need.

If you give a hungry baby a cuddle rather than the food they need, they would simply get real with you: they would actively and continuously seek what they need until they get it.

Unlike successful babies, most adults like what they see simply because they do not see what they like. They give up and settle for less. They settle for what they do not like or need rather than do the helpful baby-like thing and keep on keeping on until they get what they personally really need. However, **like babies, successful people do not like what they see if they do not see what they like**.

Just as successful adults are baby-like, successful adults are childlike also.

BEING CHILDLIKE

The child is father of the man.
(S. Smiles)

I know one thing for sure: I would not undermine the significant new things that I have learnt and continue to learn from children.

I started my professional career as a teacher at a primary school. As I write this book, I currently teach a children's class called Super Church in my local church. I teach the six to nine year-old children to become super adults and I learn from them qualities of super children. Super teachers undergo a learning experience also whilst teaching other people.

The Ratified Evidence About Life reveals that:

SUPER CHILDREN GROW UP TO BECOME SUPER ADULTS AND SUPER ADULTS 'GROW DOWN' TO BECOME 'SUPER CHILDREN'.

The principle of 'growing up' and 'growing down' would be further discussed in a subsequent section of this book that deals with my GROWTH strategy for success.

There are adults who do things that you would normally expect only a child to do; and there are children who do things that you would normally expect only an adult to do. Do you know or know of any adult who plays on sand, perhaps by the seaside during the summer? Do you know or know of a child who has put forward a wonderful idea, tackled a difficult problem, saved their own life or someone else's' life, designed a web site, or done something else that most people would normally associate with an adult?

LEARNING FROM CHILDREN

As I have stated already, successful children learn from successful adults and successful adults learn from successful children also.

I am grateful to the children I have worked with as well as the children I currently work with for teaching me a lot of things that form an integral part of the real secret of success.

I used to believe that each grey hair we have represents a diploma from the university of life. I no longer believe this. The worrying danger of saying each grey hair represents a diploma from the university of life is that the more grey hair – or diplomas – you have the more 'qualified' you are in life. There are many foolish adults out there just as there are many wise children in the world.

In an article that I wrote on age discrimination in 1996 for *Professional Manager*, a journal of the Institute of Management in the United Kingdom, I reported that:

> *"There was considerable emphasis in the past on the value of age and the experience possessed by older people. Experience was often defined quantitatively; that is by reference to 'X' number of years. Each grey hair representing a diploma from the university of life. This gave older people a competitive advantage in the recruitment process."*

In that article, I examined the nature of discrimination on grounds of age; namely, discrimination against older people, who, previously, enjoyed a competitive advantage in the recruitment process and at work just because they were older and had lots of 'diplomas' or 'grey power' from the university of life.

With regard to explaining the causes of the discrimination that was reversed against older people, I noted in the previously mentioned article that:

"The discrimination currently experienced by older workers is due to a number of factors including a redefinition of recruitment criteria by many selectors. For example, 20 years' experience is now seen by some selectors as one year's experience repeated 20 times; and you do not have to repeat a task twenty times to gain the experience required. The shift from a quantitative to a qualitative definition of experience has had an adverse impact on the value of older employees. With the advent of today's competency-based job descriptions, emphasis seems to be on how well one can do a job, not how long one has been doing it".

The key point that I would like to deal with in connection with the issues being discussed here is the phrase *'how well'* one does something – not *'how long'* one has been doing it. Learning should be determined on the basis of *'how well'*, not *'how long'*.

The fact that someone is older than you and has more grey hair does not necessarily mean that you alone should learn from them. Whilst you should learn from them the things they do well, they should also learn from you the things you do well no matter the differences in age.

Based on the preceding principle, I strongly believe that there are lots of things that an adult can and should learn from a child and a baby – and vice versa – because, like adults, children and babies have a life also; and living life is the only thing that we all have in common. **Successful people know that in order to succeed in life they have to learn from other people in the same 'trade' as themselves. All of us – babies, children and adults – are in the same business of life**.

Some of the qualities associated with being childlike are key qualities associated with the real secret of success. The examples set out in the section following would indicate to you the usefulness of learning from children.

DO CHILDLIKE THINGS

I did an unusual childlike thing when I crossed out some words in my dictionaries.

Adults may highlight words or sentences that they find interesting in books. Children cross out words or whole passages in books.

In a childlike – and definitely not childish – way I have crossed out some words in my dictionaries including the following words: defeat, devil, failure, fear, impossible, and so on. The real point being made here is not that I think these words are not proper English words; rather, my point is that I simply just do not believe in those words. And why should anyone? We must use helpful words.

On the other hand, I have identified various empowering words and have highlighted them in my dictionaries including the following empowering words arranged in alphabetical order: faith, God, Jesus Christ, positive, possible, real, success, and so on. Successful people effectively use word power.

In the section following, I invite you to be childlike and do a childlike thing. Identify some examples of words that *you* personally feel have disempowered or empowered you in life. Write down the words in the spaces provided in the section on the exercise on effectively using word power.

You could include the names of people who have considerably influenced and shaped your life *for better* – and you want to continue to let their influence guide you to success; or *for worse* – and you must stop their negative influence on your life as their impact on you drags you to failure.

Exercise: Effectively Using Word Power

Disempowering Words	Empowering Words
1.	1.
2.	2.
3.	3.
4.	4.

- You should cross out your 'disempowering words' in your dictionary if they are in your dictionary as a sign that you no longer wish to be influenced by the words.
- Highlight your 'empowering words' in your dictionary if they are in your dictionary. Write them down on a sheet of paper and repeat them to yourself at least three times right now as a way of affirming your personal belief in the words. Focus on the words carefully and for each word, remind yourself of at least one situation in which the word has previously personally empowered you.

Well done.

You would find that when next you use your dictionary and 'suddenly' find a word you highlighted or crossed out in your dictionary you would feel happy even if you did not search for the particular word in your dictionary. Just coming across the words that you previously highlighted or crossed out in your dictionary would remind you of why you either crossed them out or highlighted them and this would bring a feeling of warmth and reassurance to your mind.

When you come across such words in your dictionary, you would find that both the 'disempowering words' and the 'empowering words' would empower you. This is so because you would get a sense of joy from seeing your 'disempowering words' crossed out of your personal vocabulary as well as from seeing your 'empowering words' highlighted in your personal language of life.

When you see a 'disempowering word' that you have crossed out in your dictionary – for example, the word 'impossible' – just recall that real people in our real world have shown that the 'disempowering word' is a 'false' word. Disempowering words such as the word 'impossible' are false and misleading words because life has shown them to be false and utterly misleading. **Nothing is truly impossible to a willing heart**.

When you see an 'empowering word' that you have highlighted in your dictionary, just get real and remind yourself that the word has previously helped you or other people; and then use the word to empower yourself to move forward in life.

DO WHAT YOU ENJOY AND ENJOY WHAT YOU DO

It should be noted that children at play are not playing about; their games should be seen as their most serious-minded activity.
(Montaigne)

Another key thing associated with the real secret of success with regard to being childlike is that children enjoy playing. Like children, successful adults really enjoy playing also.

Successful adults are playful. They see work as play and they play as they work. They turn work into play and turn play into work. In this context, the word 'work' does not only refer to your professional career. Rather, it refers generally to the various things that we are engaged in doing in life. For example, parenting is work just as friends or people in a relationship have to *work* on building their relationship. In this context also, playing does not refer to a 'play ground kind of thing'; rather it refers to an activity that you enjoy doing.

Successful people do what they enjoy and enjoy what they do. They do what they like and like what they do. And they turn work into fun and fun into work.

William Shakespeare put it in a very interesting way: *to business that we love, we rise betimes, and go to it with delight*. Noel Coward also put it in an equally interesting way: *work is much more fun than fun*. As I write this book I do not *feel* that I am working. I am just having fun. Honestly! I am really enjoying myself here.

Be childlike. If, like children, you do what you enjoy and enjoy what you do, and if you turn play into work and work into play, although, sometimes you might feel tired, you would never *feel* stressed. Stress is associated with your spirit and your soul or mind; tiredness is associated with your body. Everybody could feel tired but not everybody is stressed.

In order to excel in any area of life, you must abide by a crucial law of life: do what you enjoy and enjoy what you do.

This childlike principle is associated with our individual talents and calling and would be further developed in a subsequent Chapter of this book as part of my *GROWTH* approach to personal success.

Many people do not excel at the things they do as parents, husbands, wives, singers, teachers, scholars, carers, and so on, only because they are doing something they don't enjoy doing. You don't have to be a parent or a husband or a wife or a singer or a teacher or any other thing in this world just because other people are those things. You are *you* not other people. You must know your own unique talents and calling and do your own thing in life in order to succeed.

There is no such thing as identical twins in the field of personal success. Everyone has his or her own life and unique talents and calling.

You might ask: '*But how would I know whether or not I could be a successful parent, singer, teacher or anything else, if I do not first try it out*'?

When you get real you would know that there are things in life that you don't experiment with or try out; and you would also definitely know what you would enjoy even without first trying it out.

To find out if you could personally *know* what you would enjoy without first trying it out, I invite you to examine the following short list of foods eaten by people of different cultural backgrounds and tick the ones that you personally would enjoy eating: birds, carrots, chicken, cricket and other insects, dog, uncooked fish, frog, Hedgehog, lizards, monkeys, snakes, snails, squirrel, worms.

If the list in the preceding paragraph were extended, you would definitely identify more than one thing that you would not enjoy eating, if you have not identified them already!

Successful people are not resource wasters. They concentrate their resources – time, energy, and so on – on the things that they enjoy and about which they can excel in life.

I am not saying in any way that we should not be adventurous and try out new or different things in life, although there are unsound things that we should not attempt doing; for example, trying out different ways to kill yourself or other people. Rather, what I am saying is that **we can excel in life and achieve maximum results with minimum effort when we do what we enjoy and enjoy what we do**.

A successful child knows what they are good at and would enjoy doing even before engaging in it. As a childlike person, you should engage in something that you enjoy and then enjoy what you are engaged in.

If you do not enjoy parenting, then please do not bring forth babies into the world and then abandon them or dump them in a rubbish bin as some so-called 'parents' have done. If you enjoy parenting, you would know how many children you would enjoy having and bringing up. In order to excel at parenting, you should not have more children than you would enjoy having and bringing up. Real parents know what I am talking about!

If you do not enjoy marriage, please do not get married to someone and make their life miserable; and then get married to another person afterwards, and waste that other life also, and so on.

If you do not enjoy having money, you must not have what you don't enjoy having. A friend of mine who lives in South London told me about a year ago that a woman who lived in South London at the time won a lottery jackpot; but she ended up in a psychiatric hospital just after the money was paid to her. She could not handle millions of pounds and should not have sought something that she could not handle!

The principle described in the preceding passage is a crucial law of life and an essential aspect of the real secret of success in life: doing what you are capable of enjoying and enjoying what you do.

If you do what you enjoy and enjoy what you do, you would have the motivation to move forward even when the going gets tough. When you face serious challenges in any area of life, you would give up if you were not doing what you enjoy and enjoying what you were doing.

On the other hand, you would find a way to move forward in life when you face challenges where you have the will to move forward. The will to move forward and to give up giving up is strongly associated with doing what you enjoy and enjoying what you do.

THE SKY'S NOT THE LIMIT: YOU ARE!

You must have heard of the informal expression that describes the highest level of attainment: *the sky's the limit*.

In a significant sense, *you* are the real limit to how high you can go in life. Aim to achieve excellence in whatever you do in life. When you excel in life and are the best you could possibly be, you really could get sky-high and the people that you deal with in life would applaud and praise you to the skies.

As a businessman, I know for sure that in business, money is not everything. Excellence is. And this is true in the business of life also. In order to succeed in life, you must excel in what you do. You would excel in life only if you do what you enjoy and enjoy what you do. If you break this important law of life, you would personally imprison or confine yourself to a state of failure.

HAVE CHILDLIKE IDEAS

Children often come up with wonderful ideas. Nobody can ever succeed in life without having an idea. In order to succeed in life, you must be creative; you must be someone who creatively develops childlike ideas.

Unfortunately, some adults describe wonderful childlike ideas as rubbish. As I write this passage, I have just recalled in my mind, the case of someone who once described his wife as mad because she came up with a wonderful creative idea that they should buy their own property. Initially, he described his wife's idea as rubbish, but today, the man is enjoying the property like mad!

Childlike ideas are important ideas not rubbish! In order to come up with great ideas, just let your mind freely think of different ideas like the mind of a child. Do not suppress the child in you.

As a family, my wife and I together with our two young sons have regular meetings to discuss our family business. Although we talk to each other on a daily basis including on the telephone whenever anyone of us is away from home, unlike most families, we also set aside specific times for our formal family meetings. During such times, we switch off the televisions, put the telephones on the answering machine mode to receive all incoming calls in order to avoid interruptions and so on, and then conduct a proper business-like meeting with specific agenda items regarding our family.

My wife and I duly take seriously any wonderful ideas our two young children come up with. Some very important decisions that we have made as a family and about which we have been totally happy have been based on great ideas put forward by the *really young ones* in our family as Michael Jackson described young children.

HAVE A CHILDLIKE VISION

Our son – Chidi – said recently that he needed to keep 'important rubbish'. When I first heard that phrase, I did not understand what he meant by it, so I asked him to explain to me what he meant by 'important rubbish'. He then explained to me that he could make things such as 'cars', models, 'motorbikes', and so on, from the things that we throw away as rubbish. And he does!

When my wife and I buy something in a cardboard box or a carton and then remove what we see as the important item from the cardboard box or carton, like most adults, as far as we are concerned, the empty cardboard box or carton should go into the rubbish bin. Chidi does not take that view.

We see an empty cardboard box or carton and then put it in the rubbish bin; but when our son looks at the same empty cardboard box or carton he 'sees' a model of motorbikes, cars and other things that he then makes out of the empty boxes that we throw away. Chidi has successfully designed various models including award-winning items at school from 'important rubbish'.

To 'see' is to have a vision. We do not see with our eyes; we see with our mind's eyes. Because successful people have a vision, they don't like what they see if they don't see what they like.

When I studied economics at university, we referred to the use of 'raw materials' in the process of production. What every manufacturer in the world does is to turn something that economists and other people call a 'raw material' into excellent finished products.

The phrase 'raw material' is the generally acceptable phrase for important rubbish just as the phrase 'minimum wage' is the generally acceptable way of telling employers to avoid calling their staff slaves even where they *use* their staff.

Many successful organisations in various parts of the world actually have a policy to collect and then use or reuse 'important rubbish' or recycled items.

As a family we collect and then keep important rubbish for our local authority. As with other local councils, our local authority advises people to dump their important rubbish at various collection points. The rubbish is then collected and recycled. Today, papers are made from recycled paper rubbish; glass is made from recycled broken bottles; cars are made from recycled 'rubbish' metals; and so on.

When someone first came up with the wonderful or childlike idea to recycle things, I believe that other people must have told them that their idea was rubbish. Yes, it was 'rubbish' when they first came up with their wonderful and unique idea; but look around you today and you should find excellent products that various successful people and companies have developed from ideas that initially were considered as 'rubbish'.

A form of rubbish that you must agree with me is truly a very challenging form of rubbish is sewage rubbish. Successful people truly turn 'rubbish' including sewage rubbish into something useful!

When I served on the Executive Committee of the Central and Westminster Branch of the Institute of Management in the United Kingdom, members of the Executive Committee and many top business executives from large and successful companies in the City and Westminster area of London were given a treat to visit the London Sewers. The purpose of the visit was to see how the sewage system was constructed and how it works. That was really an eye-opening treat for me.

When we arrived at the sewage yard, we were given protective clothing to wear before we went underground. When we got underground, we stood and walked in water on which was floating sewage from various parts of London. I do not wish to describe here what we saw floating on water in which we stood; but you could imagine what they looked like!

Our visit was praised and published in the institute's magazine. For me, and indeed for my colleagues that I spoke to during and after the visit, one of the most fascinating things about visiting the London sewer was that the list of people who had previously visited it included the names of people that you would not normally expect to go to such a place.

When I carefully examined the list of the people who had previously visited the sewer I noticed that the list of visitors to the place included top business people from multi-national companies, and so on. You may wonder why a top business executive of a multi-million pounds company would leave the comfort of their executive offices to spend time in a sewer; in water that contained real rubbish from various parts of London!

The simple reason for visiting the sewer was that it enabled us to appreciate success and to appreciate what successful people can do in life. We were shown fine and fascinating engineering work and how successful people recycle – real rubbish – water and turn it into useful water. At the end of our visit to the London sewer, I concluded that:

SUCCESSFUL PEOPLE TURN IMPORTANT RUBBISH INCLUDING SEWAGE RUBBISH INTO SOMETHING THAT BENEFITS THEM AND OTHER PEOPLE.

The starting point for turning anything into something that is valuable in life is to be childlike. In order to succeed in life,

you must let the child on the inside of you give you a wonderful idea, and then use it.

Everything in this world is based on an idea. Most of the wonderful things in the world today were once considered to be rubbish ideas by various people. Many people have reported that they have mentioned an idea to other people who simply regarded their ideas as rubbish.

In the end, the so-called 'rubbish' idea – to start a business, go to school, compete in the Olympics, get married to someone, buy a car, buy a property, become a nurse, go on holiday, do voluntary work, and so on – was turned into a success story that benefited even the people who initially described the idea as rubbish.

Most people also 'rubbish' their own ideas by suppressing the voice of the 'children' on the inside of themselves.

When you or other people tell *you* that your idea is rubbish simply get real with yourself and the other people by turning your idea into something that would benefit you and the world around you.

Successful people are creative people. They have ambition and imagination and are smart thinkers. They do not spend time with people who rubbish their ideas. Rather, they thrive in the company of other successful people who encourage them to further use their ideas rather than discouraging them with negative thoughts of failure.

You can and should turn any sound and specific idea that you have in life into something truly worthwhile by 'seeing' the wider picture. Children see the wider picture. Successful people do too! They can look at or think about something – even sewage rubbish – and visualise the good things that they can turn them into or extract from what they are looking at or thinking about.

Seeing the wider picture is called personal visioning. Where there is no vision, there is no success. In fact, people without a vision perish!

BE A CHILDLIKE QUESTIONER

The important thing is not to stop questioning. Curiosity
has its own reason for existing.
(Albert Einstein)

If there is anything that we wish to change in the child, we
should first examine it and see whether it is not something that
could better be changed in ourselves.
(Carl Gustav Jung)

**In order to succeed in life, you must ask yourself the single
most important question in your own world, namely:** *What
questions must I ask of myself in order to turn my life into a success
story?*

Remember: You were once a good questioner and should
always be a good questioner. In other words, you were once a
child and should always be childlike.

Children are truly very nosy. They ask loads of questions and
justifiably so! Children abide by an essential law of life and
anyone who wants to succeed in life must comply with the natural law of asking and receiving, namely: **Asking questions and
receiving answers**.

The Ratified Evidence About Life has revealed that there is
always an answer to every question in life and that you would
definitely receive an answer to any question you ask of yourself.
This is a natural law and nobody can change it: Ask and you
would receive. Ask any question and you will definitely receive
an answer.

When you ask other people or even when you ask God a question you are bound to receive an answer to your question. In the
context of asking God and other people questions, the answer to
a question could be *'Yes'* or *'No'* or it might take some other
forms such as *'not now'* or *'not yet'* or *'it depends on…'*. You would
definitely receive an answer to a question and the answer that
you receive to your question might be what you expect or what
you don't expect; but an answer you surely would receive.

Anyone who has brought up young children should be able to
confirm the fact that they ask nosy and curious questions. They
want to know almost everything! Some young children have
even asked how they got into their mommy's 'tummy'!

The use of questioning is one of the best ways in which people learn. Like children, successful adults use the questioning technique to drive their personal success programmes forward. They ask themselves and other people questions. For the purpose of the point being made in this passage, I would concentrate on the crucial success-directed questions that we should personally ask ourselves.

The questioning component of the real secret of success requires you to *think* and to properly think through issues. By engaging in asking questions and receiving answers to your personal questions, you would be engaging in a thorough and proper analysis of issues through the use of a proper and effective thought process. This has many advantages including the following advantages:

- You would be able to identify a range of issues associated with something that you are considering.
- You would be able to identify various options and opportunities.
- You would be able to imagine things, be creative, and generate new ideas.
- You would be able to make proper decisions.
- You would be able to weigh up different methods and identify the best way forward in any given situation.
- You would be able to tackle problems constructively rather than worrying about them.
- You would be able to know the meanings and consequences of an issue.
- You would be able to evaluate and review an action or issue.
- You would be able to see a 'bigger picture'.
- You would be able to listen to yourself, listen to other people and listen to God.
- And you would be able to do many other things.

Remember to ask yourself crucial questions. By asking crucial questions of yourself, you would apply a lateral or unusual but effective thinking approach to life. Questioning takes various forms as set out in the section following. Depending on the issue that you are dealing with, you should ask yourself crucial questions using any or a combination of the questioning techniques set out in the section following.

Closed Questions

Saying 'Yes' or 'No' normally can answer closed questions. You would find closed questions helpful in handling very specific issues that you would like to clarify.

For example, with regard to the sound and specific component of my *SMARTER* approach to setting goals, you would find it useful to ask yourself a relevant closed question: *Is this goal or proposed action legal?*

Open Questions

Open questions begin with words like 'Where', 'Who', 'When', 'What', 'How' 'Why' and so on. They enable you to examine an issue in full, expand your responses, and identify feelings, attitudes, and facts.

Examples of open questions include: *How can I improve the quality of my life? What steps are necessary to move from 'here' to 'there'? Why should I take such steps?*

Linking Questions

Linking questions enable you to form a transition from one topic or issue to another. For example you could ask *How does 'this' option relate to 'that' other one?*

Probing Questions

Probing questions are designed to enable you to dig deeper. They enable you to draw out more information from yourself. Examples include: *What else should I consider about my goal or plan? What are the other issues associated with taking 'this' action?*

General Questions

General questions would enable you to discover and clarify your understanding of an idea, or your views on a certain issue. An example is the question: *How would this action affect or benefit other people around me?*

Specific Questions

Specific questions enable you to *focus* on a very specific point or to clarify your understanding of a specific issue. An example is:

What are the issues for me regarding doing 'this' form of exercise (rather than exercising in general)?

Hypothetical Questions

Hypothetical questions are the 'If' or 'What if' questions. They enable you to look at issues from different dimensions; namely, obviously positive dimensions as well as the devil's advocate dimension. Most people think that the devil's advocate dimension is bad. It is not bad. Asking questions from the devil's advocate perspective may not obviously seem positive and acceptable to you because it takes you out of your comfort zone. However, such questions are not negative because they purposefully enable you to look at the possible consequences of things as well as the 'other side' of things that might not be obvious to you. They help you to see and deal with the blind spot aspects of your thinking process.

Examples of hypothetical questions are: *What would I do if I am promoted (or demoted) to work in another job during my company's restructuring exercise? I look to Alex to do 'this or that thing' for me; what if he or she lets me down?*

Constructive Critical Questions

Constructive self-criticism or self-feedback is a very helpful way to identify the causes of previous mistakes, tackle them head on and then move forward in life. Such questions should not be designed to put *you* down. Rather, you must pose the questions in a constructive way aimed at helping you to avoid past mistakes and identify areas of your life that require improvement. As Thomas Carlyle reminds us, *"The greatest of faults, I should say, is to be conscious of none"*.

Sometimes, you might find it helpful to ask yourself: *Why did I not achieve the result as desired? What exactly happened and what must I do differently to obtain a different result next time?* And you could even ask yourself this (more critical but helpful) question: *Where did this mess come from and what must I do to avoid it happening again?*

You must remember that constructive critical questions must be valid and fully justified questions and that they should be directed at the *issues* – or the *mess* as in the preceding example – rather than at you. You may have done something that is a mess;

but *you* are not a mess. I once told my children that they are not naughty boys, but that they had done a naughty *thing* by leaving their room untidy. We then worked together to tidy up the room and put their many toys where they should duly have been kept. A put down of yourself and other people must be avoided. The focus of constructive critical questions should be on the *thing* and how it should be prevented from happening again next time.

Reflective Questions

Reflective questions enable you to double-check or reflect on something rather than merely jumping to conclusions.

They also help you to clarify your understanding and encourage you to say more. For example, if you have just decided to travel to New York, you might further reflect on your decision by asking yourself this question: *Is travelling to New York really the best thing for me to do right now? Have I fully considered the issues associated with my decision?*

You should also use reflective questions to reflect on specific things or to reflect on your life in general. Some relevant examples of reflective questions that you might find useful in this regard include the following questions: *Am I really moving towards my destiny in life? Given that life is where everyone gets in and gets out, what would I like to be remembered for when I get out? Am I really living a good and successful life?*

Reflective questions can be linked into *evaluative questions* that enable you to evaluate or review things; for example, 'How am I getting on with my goals'? 'Is there anything that needs changing'?

Leading Questions

Leading questions are questions that indicate the required answer. For example, if you plan to celebrate success by giving yourself or other people a treat you could ask yourself: *It would be nice to celebrate success, wouldn't it?*

Care should be taken not to use leading questions in a mistaken way to lead yourself to take an action that you have not properly thought through. In the example used in this passage, it should be apparent to everyone that it is definitely nice to celebrate success and you would be fully justified to lead yourself in the direction of celebrating success by asking questions that deliberately lead you to celebrate success!

REAL QUESTIONS ARE THE REAL ANSWERS

Asking real questions is the real answer to the questions we have in life. You would never find an answer to anything if you do not ask a question about it. A question would generate an answer.

The law of cause and effect is a law of life that nobody can change. Something causes something. *Just as a fire produces smoke, so do questions produce answers.*

There is a complementary relationship between 'cause' and 'effect'. Less fire produces less smoke and more fire produces more smoke. More questions produce more answers and fewer questions produce fewer answers. Similarly, real questions produce real answers.

Questions and answers are like fire and smoke. Where there is fire there is definitely smoke and when you fire questions at yourself you would definitely smoke out the hidden or previously unknown answers to your problems.

You would never find an answer to any problem in life if you do not ask a question about it. In a real sense, asking real questions is the real answer to life's real problems. *If you are struggling with any situation or want an answer to any problem in life, the answer to your situation or problem lies in asking the right questions.*

Remember, every question has an answer. And when you ask unusual and new questions, you would receive unusual and new answers.

When you use the success-directed questioning techniques set out in the preceding passages, you would purposefully take your personal success programme forward.

By asking the right questions and receiving the right answers, you can make a fresh statement about your own life and turn your life into a remarkable success story.

> *If I could see the world through the eyes of a child, ... what a wonderful world this would be.*
> (Patsy Cline)

Don't be deceived by 'grown-ups'. When you look at an adult on the outside, you see a 'grown-up' person; but on the inside of every successful adult are a baby and a child. *You* would

never succeed in life if you suppress or ignore the baby and the child in you.

Succeeding in life is like climbing a ladder. When you move up to a higher step or rung on the ladder of life, you must not chop off the ones underneath. If you do, you would never get to the top let alone stay there.

Many so-called 'grown up' people do not succeed in staying on top of life only because in the process of growing up, they chop off their baby-like and childlike supportive stages on the ladder of life.

Get real right now and make a fresh start today by reviving the baby and the child on the inside of you.

8

WAYS OF LIFE AND RESPONSES TO LIFE'S CHALLENGES

Life is like a sewer. What you get out of it depends on what you put into it.
(Tom Lehrer)

Through focusing on your life, taking a snapshot of it and then developing the negatives in your life, you would have a picture of the aspects of your life that you hate. You should redirect the powerful emotion of hatred and positively use it to change your life from worse to better.
(Innocent Izamoje)

Our ways of life including our attitudes to life shape and determine our destinies.

I would like to illustrate this point by using an example that I have found to be very popular with the numerous people to whom I have mentioned it on various training courses and seminars. I would actively engage you in doing this by means of an exercise.

I ask you to carry out the exercise below. Please think through each stage of the exercise and do what you are requested to do at each stage before proceeding to the next stage.

Exercise: Tackling The Lion

Stage 1:
Imagine that you have just returned home from work or from visiting a friend, or from carrying out any other outdoor activity. You are now standing by your front door. Please visualise yourself standing in front of your front door. Just stay there for a moment. Now, read the instruction contained in Stage 2 below.

Stage 2:
Visualise yourself reaching out for the key to your front door. Do not open your door. Just visualise yourself reaching out for the key to your front door as you stand by your front door. Fine, you now have the key in your hands.

Stage 3:
Then visualise yourself gently opening your front door. Don't go in yet. Just gently open the door, but please don't go in yet.

Stage 4:
Now, gently go in. As you open your door and take your first step into your property, you see the fierce-looking lion on your hallway. The lion is roaring and approaching you.

QUESTION: What would you do?

Please write down your response to the above question in the space provided below:

_____

_____

I describe the preceding exercise as *'the Lion Metaphor and the Five 'F' Responses'*. I developed and constructed the exercise after duly analysing and adapting a biblical assertion about the roaring lion roaming around and looking for someone to devour!

Different people respond to the scenario specified in the *'Lion Metaphor'* exercise in different ways. All the responses to the question can be put into various categories which I call the *'Five 'F' Responses'*; namely, the:

Flight response
Fall response
Freeze response
Flow response
Fight response.

The lion-on-the-hallway exercise enables us to identify our primary way of life. The issue about our ways of life is discussed later on in this Chapter. At this stage, I would like to analyse the various responses.

FLIGHT RESPONSE

Most people who respond to the lion-on-the-hallway metaphor or illustration offer a *flight* response and say that they would run away from the lion.

Some people reading this passage might reply: '*I don't blame people who say that they would run away from the lion on their hallway. Who can stand or tackle the lion? Who, with a sound mind, would like to tackle the lion? And why should they tackle the lion, anyway?*'

If you have a tendency to say the sort of things specified above, I would ask you to seriously think again about the validity of your response by carefully analysing the questions set out in the section following. Remember: *real questions produce real answers*! Therefore, consider the following real questions and find the real answers to them:

- Do you really think that running away from the lion is the best way to respond to the situation?
- Do you know of any person who has taken on and successfully defeated the lion on their hallway?
- Could you think of at least one example where *you* have personally taken on and successfully defeated the lion on your hallway? Another way of putting this question is to ask: Could you think of at least one example where you have personally taken on and successfully overcome any problem or obstacle that seemed to block or stop you from achieving something in life as desired?

At this stage, you should know or at least have a rough idea about where I am coming from and where I am taking you.

As I have stated already, most people who have personally responded to my lion-on-the-hallway exercise at various seminars offer a *flight* response.

Doing a *flight* is the typical approach applied by most people to problems and obstacles in life. When most people are confronted by any problem – *the lion* – they offer a flight response. They simply give up and run away from tackling problems!

Most people do not tackle their personal problems head on. Instead, they manufacture all kinds of excuses for not taking the necessary steps to tackle their personal problems.

Committing suicide is the worst and most extreme form of *flight* **response to life's challenges.**

Unfortunately, rather than tackle life's challenges head on, some people take a *flight* away from life altogether. YOU don't need to do that. The Ratified Evidence About Life has revealed that you can and would enjoy life if YOU personally want and choose to.

Successful people do not *do a runner*. **The 'lion' or a problem stands no chance with them.**

As well as taking a flight response by running away from the lion, some people have gone as far as saying that they would not even look twice at the lion before running away from it; and that they would not return to their properties because they *fear* the lion on their hallway. This point simply means that they do not look twice at their personal problems in life and never attempt to go back and tackle problems because they *fear* they would not succeed in tackling their personal problems.

MORE THAN THE LION'S SHARE OF YOUR OWN LIFE

Personal success is not about having the lion's share. No way!

I have heard people say that you *'win some and lose some'* in life. People who apply this misguided philosophy to life say it does not really matter to them if they fail as a parent or in their relationships providing they succeed in another area of their life such as their professional career.

I do not know how many parts or roles you personally have to your own life; but my life comprises of various parts including the following: husband, father, extended family, friends, paid work, voluntary work, church activities, leisure activities, relaxation, learning and continuing personal development, and so on. I am seeking actively and continuously to succeed in ALL areas of my life rather than settling for the lion's share.

Nobody should assign any number of roles or parts to your life or misinform you that you must have exactly 'X' number of roles or parts to your life. You and you alone should decide the exact number of parts or roles in your life that you can cope with and enjoy; and how big or small each part should be in line with your own reality and enjoyment. For example, do you personally want to be a parent? If so, you should then decide how big or small you want that role to be: Do you want two or ten children?

On some of my personal development training courses, I ask the training course participants to list the various parts or roles in their lives and then decide if and how they should increase or reduce the number of roles that they are engaged in to reflect the changes in their own realities or circumstances.

You would find it beneficial to carry out the exercise below.

Exercise: Life roles or parts

- List your various roles or the various parts to your life. Be honest with yourself as you do the list.
- Look again at what you have come up with. Think it through.
- Do you like what you see? If your answer is 'Yes' then you do not have an immediate need to change the various components of your life. If your answer is 'No' then you have an immediate need to change your life; and you should change it right now!

There are two main ways of considering changing the various parts of your life. You can increase or reduce the number of parts depending on your reality, priorities, needs, and so forth. Sometime ago, I decided to resign from serving on some Executive Committees within my professional organisations in order to reallocate my time and other resources to other activities or parts of my life.

You can also increase or decrease the amount of time and other resources you commit to any part of your life at any particular moment even if you do not increase or decrease the number of roles you personally carry out in life.

What the Ratified Evidence About Life has shown is that in order to live a good quality life, you should have various aspects to your life. A variety of roles in life can add real spice to your life! On the other hand, you should not take on too many roles that you cannot cope with.

You can and should successfully live life. Life should not be about seeking to succeed in some areas and then settling for failure in other areas. You can tackle and overcome the 'lion' in your life when you get real; and you can successfully enjoy all of your life rather than merely settling for the lion's share.

THE MEANING OF THE LION METAPHOR

It depends on what the meaning of 'is' is.
(Bill Clinton)

I have used '*the lion*' as a symbol of the problems or obstacles that hinder you from succeeding in whatever you are engaged in doing in life. In other words, the lion represents the road-blocks on your road to success.

'*You*' refers to you personally with regard to whether or not you personally take responsibility for your own success in life. '*The lion is roaring and approaching you*' indicates that problems come to people even if they do not do anything to attract problems in life. The lion is '*fierce-looking*' indicates that some problems in life might seem to overwhelm you because they seem impossible to deal with.

The point regarding '*imagining*' that you have just returned home to see the lion on your hallway indicates that fear is often based on 'evidence' or 'expectations' that are imagined rather than real. I will come back to this point when I discuss 'fear approach' to life. '*Visualising yourself reaching out for the key to your front door, gently opening your door and going in*' indicate visualising yourself taking steps to move forward in life.

Your '*hallway*' represents your road to success; that is, the process of getting into your 'property'. Your '*property*' represents your goal and the accomplishment of your vision or destiny in life.

The '*key in your hand*' that you used to unlock '*your front door*' is your proper understanding and use of the real secret of success offered to you in this book that would enable you to unlock and gain access to personal success in life. Your '*front door*' represents your commencement of your journey of success.

Having the 'key' or opening the 'door' is not enough. You have to DO other things including effectively tackling the lion on your hallway in order to succeed and enjoy your 'property'. In other words, just understanding the real secret of success is not enough. You must continue to get real and properly apply it.

With regard to properly applying my parable or metaphor, I would like to ask you to note that I referred to overcoming '*the lion*' – a symbolic lion – rather than 'a lion'. You should in no way seek to tackle or physically overcome a lion. People who get real understand what I am talking about!

A few years ago, newspapers and various radio and television news reports reported the story of a young man who climbed over the protective barriers at a Zoo and threw himself into the area of the Zoo in which wild animals including lions were kept. He was lucky to be alive after being rescued by workers at the Zoo. It was also reported that the young man stated that he read a story about someone called Daniel who triumphed in a lion's den very many years ago. It was further reported that the man had a form of mental illness.

According to the news reports, the young man also stated that he personally wanted to prove that, like Daniel, he too could overcome a lion. This was a terrible and mistaken application of information and people who get real don't do such a daft thing!

FALL RESPONSE

Some people respond to my lion parable or metaphor by saying that they would slump when they see the roaring lion approaching them on their hallway. Some people's self-confidence drops as a result of facing challenges in life.

A key difference between people who offer a flight response and those who offer a *fall* response to life's challenges is that those who offer a flight response avoid tackling a problem – the lion. They might even do the extreme form of flight response – commit suicide – rather than face problems especially humiliating problems.

Those who offer a fall response do not run away from problems or move forward either. When presented with problems in life, they simply mentally fall down, stay down, and are then destroyed or weakened by the problems they fail to destroy. When you hear someone say that he or she is feeling low or that he or she has a low self-esteem, it means they have *fallen* down in response to life's challenges or have been knocked down by life's challenges.

FREEZE RESPONSE

In a way, the fall response is similar to the *freeze* response. When some people are presented with problems in life they personally enlarge the problems as a result of the way in which they see the problem and then *freeze*. With regard to handling personal problems in life, some people see a mountain rather than a molehill.

People who offer a freeze response to situations in life are likely to have a nervous breakdown. They might seem to be solid mentally and it might seem as though they are coping with problems; however, they suddenly crack up just as solid ice breaks into pieces in a hot environment! Unfortunately, although some of them recover, many are completely frozen out of the journey of life because they permanently lose it!

People who freeze in response to life's challenges are ice-bound or frozen in, and they never succeed in life. As my *GROWTH* strategy – discussed in a subsequent section of this book – demonstrates, success in life is about 'growth'. Nothing grows in ice!

FLOW RESPONSE

Many people have responded to my lion-on-the-hallway exercise by saying that they would simply go with the *flow* dictated by the lion.

People who 'go with the flow' in life let 'the lion' or life's problems call the shots and they do not do anything positively to determine their own destinies. Problems control them. They do not exercise control over their own problems and over their own destinies. With regard to the journey of life, they are happy being passengers rather than drivers.

What a thing it is to merely go with the flow of the journey of life rather than personally determining that flow as successful people do!

Some people *go with the flow* in various misdirected ways. There are people who live their lives just by imitating other people; or by doing something because of peer group pressure; or by living their lives in a particular way to impress other people, for example, buying a big brand new car on hire purchase just to impress other people without telling the other people that they bought the big brand new car on hire purchase!

FIGHT RESPONSE

If you fight and run away, you live to fight another day.
(Bob Marley)

A small number of people – always the minority of those who respond to my lion-on-the-hallway exercise – say that they would apply the *fight* response.

As well as saying that they do not feel that they should give up their property to the lion, they also argue that it is their right to enjoy their property and that the lion would not stop them from exercising that right. In other words, they would exercise their right to succeed in life and would not be detracted or overwhelmed by any problem.

Whenever I check with people on training courses how they would *fight* the symbolic lion on their hallway, they normally indicate that they would not fight the lion on their own because they don't have to do that. They say they would use everything they have including their own strong will and motivation to fight the lion; their friends, colleagues, neighbours, or anyone who can help them in fighting the lion; any 'weapon' that they can gain access to that might be of help to them in fighting the lion; and so on.

This response demonstrates a key aspect of the real secret of success: **As well as helping themselves, successful people also seek help from other sources, including other people**. **Successful people FIGHT their way through life in order to get on.**

Remember: Life is about getting in, getting on and getting out! Everyone gets in and would definitely get out. But not everyone gets on. Only people who get real and apply a fight response to life's challenges actually GET ON.

The Ratified Evidence About Life shows that **Successful people are not quitters because quitters are not successful people**.

WAYS OF LIFE

The five 'F' responses described in the preceding passage are instinctively induced by two 'F' ways of life; namely, a *fear* way of life and a *faith* way of life.

At different times in life and depending on the issues (lion) that you are dealing with, most people – definitely, not everybody – might have both a fear and a faith way of life. The same person might apply a fear approach to one thing and a faith approach to another thing. And the same person might apply a fear approach to one thing one day and then apply a faith approach to the same thing the next day.

Whilst some people might switch between a fear and a faith approach, others just apply only a fear or a faith approach to life.

It is possible to know your own *primary way of life*; that is, the kind of person you instinctively are in all or most situations. This is the *real* you. Some people are instinctively driven by fear whereas others are instinctively driven by faith. Some people who, initially, respond to situations by means of fear, change their approach to a faith approach later on; and vice versa.

Some people respond to situations by means of a fear approach and never change their approach to life just as some – successful – people respond to situations by means of a faith approach and never change their approach to life to a fear-directed one.

I know of many examples where people think about commencing a project or have been given a piece of work to do; and instinctively they immediately replied that they could not handle it. However, when they started working on the task, they realised that the task was not as difficult as they feared initially.

Because of their primary fear approach to life, many people condemn themselves as having failed even before starting a project.

First impressions last! The first impressions that you form about a situation would last a long time; and the *effect* on you of your first impressions could last a very long time indeed.

It is very helpful in life to get it right first time and nowhere is this principle more relevant than to our ways of life. Therefore, the first and the only way of life that we should have is a faith approach to life.

Exercise: Identifying your own way of life

- What is your approach to life: *faith* approach or *fear* approach?

The best way to answer the question above is to go back to your answer regarding the lion-on-the-hallway exercise.

If your answer to the lion-on-the-hallway exercise was to fight the lion, then you have the right and empowering faith approach to life.

If your answer was to run away or if you offered a 'fall', 'freeze' or 'flow' response, you have a negative and disempowering fear approach to life and must change that approach right now.

If you initially or instinctively said that you would do a flight, fall, freeze or flow but then changed your mind to fight the lion on the hallway, your primary way of life is a fear approach; but you have made a purposeful and helpful change already by now having a faith approach. Well done!

Remember: In order to succeed and continue to succeed, you should only apply a faith approach to situations.

FEAR

We have nothing to fear but fear itself.
(Franklin Roosevelt)

The only thing I am afraid of is fear.
(Duke of Wellington, "The Iron Duke")

Fear is that little darkroom where negatives are developed.
(Michael Pritchard)

Fear is both physically and mentally disabling.
(Innocent Izamoje)

Like faith, fear is also a very powerful emotion.

Unlike babies and very young children, every adult has the capacity to fear. The most crucial point about fear as an emotion is that we should control it rather than be controlled by it. As an emotion, 'fear' warns us of potential or actual dangers in order for us to pause, fully analyse and reflect on the dangers and then act to avoid them.

Fear should not suppress or stop us. We must immediately eliminate fear from our thought processes once it has served its only useful purpose of warning us of a potential or actual danger. Fear would suppress us if we do not eliminate it from our thought processes.

In the context of our approaches to life, fear is represented by the abbreviation *FEAR* that stands for:

> **F**alse
> **E**vidence (or Expectation)
> **A**ppearing
> **R**eal.

I heard the description of FEAR on a radio broadcast. I really liked it when I heard it: **F**alse **E**vidence (or **E**xpectation) **A**ppearing **R**eal. Whoever constructed that description of fear deserves to be praised.

I have in the past been paralysed by fear. I know exactly the serious negative effects of fear on people who fail to develop the capacity to tackle fear. I would cite a personal example to illustrate this point.

My wife, children and I regularly visit our extended families in Nigeria. On one occasion, I developed a very strong and overwhelming but misinformed sense of fear. My fear was based on the false evidence that did not just seem real, but seemed very real at the time.

Before we embarked on our journey on the occasion referred to, I was terrified by the news of armed robbers attacking people in Nigeria. In the same year that we were due to travel to Nigeria, my immediate younger brother was attacked during an incident in which seven police officers that confronted the armed robbers were killed. Armed robbers also attacked our family home on two separate occasions and robbed my mother of her possessions. Armed robbers attacked one of my younger sisters also. Another younger brother of mine also reported that armed robbers broke into the house in which he resided and attacked one of his neighbours. There were other reports of attacks on other people by armed robbers in that same year.

If you let fear control you, you would find every reason to 'justify' your fear. In my case, I had the reason or evidence of armed robbers attacking various members of my extended family, and twice attacking the property where my own family and I intended to reside in Nigeria to 'justify' my fear. In the end, the evidence, which seemed real, was absolutely false. My holiday was spoilt not by armed robbers but by fear.

Rather than apply a fear approach to the holiday, I could have applied a faith approach and then seen what I wanted to see before and during the holiday.

If I had applied a faith approach, I could have *seen* the following real facts: that I grew up in Nigeria and was never attacked by armed robbers when I resided in Nigeria; that more members of my extended family were not attacked by armed robbers than were attacked in the year in question; that I had previously safely visited Nigeria on many occasions but was attacked by armed robbers only on one occasion in 1985; that I had also previously safely visited Nigeria on many occasions after being attacked by armed robbers there in 1985; that there are about one hundred and ten million people safely living in Nigeria; that I could have done something to enhance our security during our holiday in Nigeria rather than worrying about it; that people get attacked all over the world; that one of the greatest issues being dealt with by the British Home Secretary and the Metropolitan Police Service in London where I reside is the increasing level of crime in London; and so on.

What fear and faith ways of life lead you to do in life is this: you would mentally *see* exactly what you want to see in life and what you mentally see would then determine how you live your life and how you live your life would determine what you see physically. Faith and fear create a self-fulfilling prophecy.

FAITH

You will become as small as your controlling desire; as great as your dominant aspiration.
(James Allen)

We are not interested in the possibilities of defeat; they do not exist.
(Queen Victoria)

I came, I saw, I conquered.
(Julius Caesar)

Everyone who has come into this world must conquer failure; and a crucial way to conquer failure is to conquer fear through the effective application of a faith approach to life.

People with a *faith* approach to life apply a fight response to problems and situations. In this context, the word faith represents the abbreviation: FAITH.

I have constructed the abbreviation FAITH in a three-dimensional way to reflect the three usefully integrated parts that make up our lives and that enable us to activate and achieve success in life: *spirit*, *soul* and *body*. My model of faith is reported in the section following.

PART ONE: *Spirit.* At our 'spirit' level, FAITH means:

> **F**earlessly
> **A**ctivated
> **I**nwardly
> **T**hrough
> **H**ope

PART TWO: *Soul.* With regard to our 'soul' FAITH means:

> **F**ocusing
> **A**head
> **I**rrespective of
> **T**he
> **H**indrances

PART THREE: *Body.* At the physical level, FAITH means:

> **F**ighting
> **A**ll
> **I**
> **T**ruly
> **H**ate.

You should note the focus on the letter 'I' in Part Three – the outcomes or results component of my three-dimensional model of faith. Our faith at the 'spirit' and 'soul' levels lead to tangible results at the 'body' level. The emphasis on the letter 'I' at the practical 'body' level shows that '*I am personally responsible for doing things to ensure my own success in life*'. By applying the 'I' philosophy, this is the way to read my three-dimensional aspect of *FAITH*:

SPIRIT: *Vital Spark*:

I am:

Fearlessly
Activated
Inwardly
Through
Hope

SOUL: *Mindset*:

Therefore, I firmly believe in success and in:

Focusing
Ahead
Irrespective of
The
Hindrances

BODY: *Doing (Activity)*:

As a result of which I am:

Fighting
All
I
Truly
Hate.

The Collins English Dictionary and Thesaurus defines the word 'spirit' as "*the force or principle of life that animates the body of living things*". This is the context in which I am using the word 'spirit'.

Similarly, with regard to the level of our 'soul' I use the expression 'focusing ahead' to reflect our motivation to move forward, increase speed and maintain our momentum for taking our success programme forward irrespective of the hindrances that we encounter on the road to success.

I would like to thank my young son – Chinwe – for helping me with the construction of my three-dimensional model of faith with regard to the aspect of the 'soul'. When I was putting the model together and seemed to be struggling with regard to the words to describe the 'soul' component, I invited him to work with me. He – a primary school pupil – helped me to think through the model at the level of the soul and suggested the word 'hindrances' to me. Indeed, successful adults learn from successful children and vice versa.

Faith is what links up and keeps our spirit, soul and body together. Your 'spirit' or *hope* to succeed activates your 'soul' thereby giving you the strong belief based on a positive mindset to *focus ahead* and this in turn activates your 'body' to *do* the things that are necessary for you to succeed.

You might previously have heard about the phrase 'spirit, soul and body'. Most religions refer to the 'spirit, soul and body', and people who study the science and art of life such as psychologists and philosophers also refer to 'spirit, soul and body' although some of them present the idea in different unfamiliar ways such as 'id', 'ego', and 'super-ego'; or 'conditioned self', 'unconditioned self' and so on.

For a long time in my life, I used the phrase 'spirit, soul and body' like most people do in a singsong way without duly considering and understanding what it means.

By carefully studying and analysing what makes people succeed in life, I have found that only people who get real succeed because they are *full of spirit* and raring to go (SPIRIT LEVEL); they have the *right spirit* (SOUL OR MINDSET LEVEL); and they play the game of life with *great spirit* as a result of which they produce a spirited performance and defeat failure (BODY LEVEL).

You must personally demonstrate faith in all three areas of your life – spirit, soul and body – in order to succeed. You must have faith in your 'sprit' with regard to HOPING to succeed; you must have faith in your 'soul' by having the right mindset that you would successfully overcome the HINDRANCES on the road to success; and you must have faith in your 'body' with regard to doing things that effectively enable you to fight and defeat something that you HATE – failure – as well as the things associated with it.

By faithfully and positively applying the emotive power of hatred, you would definitely give up giving up; and not only would you tackle and destroy the roadblocks on the road to success, you would also be seeking actively to ensure that they no longer block your way to success because you truly hate them.

I have deliberately used the emotive word 'hate' to demonstrate how successful people feel about, and then behave towards, something that seeks to derail them from succeeding. People who apply faith face up to and tackle their problems head on. They fight, fight, fight! And they fight failure because they truly hate it. **No faith, no fight.**

Given that failure comes naturally to people in that they don't have to really work hard or do anything to attract it – but definitely have to work hard and do something to avoid it – it follows that people must fight failure head on in order to prevent it. In this regard, the saying *'attack is the best form of defence'* is very appropriate. Failure is a dangerous enemy. The best way to avoid or eliminate it is to attack it; if you don't first attack and tackle failure, it would definitely attack you and overwhelm you as the lives of most people demonstrate.

How do you personally feel about something you really truly *hate*? Can you stand it or stomach it? What does your feeling drive you to do about it? And how much energy do you apply to doing it? Try honestly and seriously answering and analysing these questions and you should understand why and how people with faith who want to succeed in life fight the most important thing they truly hate: failure.

The Ratified Evidence About Life has revealed that hate and love are both extremely powerful emotions and that people are minded to DO something about what they hate or love.

The evidence also shows that **most people do not seriously and obsessively practice love to the extent that they seriously and obsessively practice hatred. Most people who say they really LOVE you could not die for you; but if they really HATE you, they could kill you!**

The above observation is a sad but factual reality of life. It is for this reason that I used the description Fighting All I Truly Hate with regard to the action level of FAITH because I want to tap into and then positively and constructively redirect the powerful emotion of hatred that most people find easier to apply to situations in life. This, I believe, is what Earl Nightingale rightly referred to as the benefit of being "constructively discontented".

There are many examples where people have successfully redirected their strong emotion of hatred and then put it into good causes with great energy.

A man called Saul really hated, attacked, and harassed Christians. When he positively and constructively redirected his hatred emotion and took on a new name as Paul he became one of the most serious supporters of Christianity; and he wrote several books in the New Testament.

In Charles Dickens' book *Christmas Carol*, Scrooge really hated Christmas. When he positively and constructively redirected his hatred emotion he became the world's most popular celebrant of Christmas in English history. Most names are not in the English dictionary. Scrooge's is!

A challenging example of redirecting hatred emotion that I heard about first-hand was the account of a young woman. She personally reported that she really hated paid work. Rather than take up a paid job, she spent her time as an unemployed layabout.

She also reported that after personally watching a wealthy man lose his wealth as a result of drug addiction, and after personally listening to the man's account in a hospital, she was really challenged. Thankfully, she met the challenge and positively and constructively redirected her previous hatred emotion against paid work in favour of paid work.

Today, the young woman referred to in this passage who previously hated paid work does a good senior-level paid job and co-ordinates a scheme for unemployed people designed to help them secure employment. What a positive change this is! On one occasion when she was advising some unemployed people who, evidently, hated paid work, I was thrilled by the following comment that she made to the group: '*I was once like you; I have been there before*'.

Most people have been there before and most people are still *there* today: in a situation where they apply the powerful emotion of hatred. What they need and should do is to positively and constructively redirect this powerful emotion of hatred and then use it to drive their success programmes forward.

If most people *love success* just for the sake of loving success, they might not take success as seriously and as far as they could if they *hate failure*. People normally activate their personal success in life if they hate failure or if they love success because they hate failure. For the few people in the world who find it easier to love than to hate, they must apply their love for success in a manner that reflects their hatred of failure also. I would further discuss this point in a subsequent section in which I deal with my HOLD therapy.

> *Walk on, walk on, with hope in your heart,*
> *And you'll never walk alone.*
> (Oscar Hammerstein II)

> *Human life begins on the far side of despair.*
> (Jean-Paul Sartre)

I developed my three-dimensional model of FAITH after duly analysing and adapting a biblical assertion that *faith is the substance of things HOPED for, the evidence of things not seen.*

Like fear that is based on evidence – which though is false evidence that appears real – faith is based on evidence also. This is the kind of evidence that I indicate by means of my abbreviation REAL: Ratified Evidence About Life.

Through the proper application of faith, you would eventually get *the substance of things HOPED for.* And the substance or outcome of what you hoped for would be the evidence that justifies your faith.

Successful people with a faith approach to life are fighters. They fight 'the lion' regardless of the way in which it presents.

They truly hate and then fight *failure* and the things associated with failure such as fear, defeat, quitting, negative thoughts, poor self-management, surrounding oneself with people with a fear approach to life, lack of planning, lack of goal setting, procrastination, indecision, laziness, impossibility thinking, low self-esteem, put-downs by self and by other people, lack of personal accountability for own actions or inactions, lack of assertiveness and personal effectiveness, and so on.

Successful people also fight against their own senses by seriously thinking things through.

Hate Or Love Discipline

You must apply a disciplined approach to life in order to succeed in life. I developed a therapeutic approach to life and have

taught many other people to use it. It really works. I developed
the principle after carefully studying what makes various
people successful. The therapy is based on the abbreviation
HOLD:

Hate
Or
Love
Discipline

The **R**atified **E**vidence **A**bout **L**ife reveals that everyone holds
on to things in life: you hold on to love or you hold on to hatred.
This is why I developed the abbreviation HOLD.

The word 'discipline' in the context of my HOLD principle or
therapy reflects its grammatical meaning with regard to
'method' or 'practice'. In other words, different people have different methods of living life; and different people practice
'hatred' or 'love'.

If it is easier for you to practice love, then use the love method
or route to drive your success programme forward.

If it is easier for you to practice hatred as it is with most
people, then use the hatred method or route to take your success
programme forward.

On the basis of the proper application of my HOLD therapy,
regardless of the method or route that you use, everyone would
arrive at the same point: *success*.

The **R**atified **E**vidence **A**bout **L**ife has revealed that it is easier
for most people to hate something than it is for them to love
something. Therefore, rather than tell you to stop doing what
seems really very deep in most people's minds – 'hating' something – I urge you to develop a very strong sense of hatred and
then positively and constructively redirect your hatred emotion.
By turning the powerful emotion of hatred into constructive and
helpful energy, you would improve your own little world and
the wider world in which we all live.

For a moment, imagine what a lovely and peaceful world we
would all have if everyone were able to *hate* war, murder, child
abuse, racism, sexism, armed robbery, rape, and all kinds of
evil!

My HOLD principle is designed to enable you to hold your
own rather than to hold you back. It is aimed at enabling you

to *hold on* to your success programme rather than to put it on hold!

You can move forward in life by loving something and then positively doing something about what you love or by hating something and then positively doing something about what you personally hate. What really matters is that you positively do something about what you love or hate. Both the person who hates war and the person who loves peace do great things for us all.

Most people think the word 'hatred' is totally bad. It is not. Even people that you personally could see as saints have emotions like every other person and they also practice hatred like every other person. However, it is good that they only *hate* **war, murder, child abuse, racism, sexism, armed robbery, rape, and other forms of evil!**

Many people have used phrases like: *'I hate this war'*; *'I hate the way in which the poor are treated'* and *'I hate the way in which animals are cruelly treated'*. Such a positive and constructive application of the powerful emotion of hatred has given rise to worthy things such as peace missions, the minimum wage and the animal rights movement.

The hate or love therapeutic principle is really crucial to personal change in life. Love is associated with pleasure and enjoyment. By just loving something you automatically focus on the enjoyment and pleasure associated with it; and you would create your own enjoyment and pleasure from doing something you really love. Therefore, you are likely to do something or continue to do something where you associate love and pleasure with it.

On the other hand, hatred is associated with disgust and pain. If you hate something, you would automatically be disgusted at it no matter the way in which it is presented. And because of your disgust at it or hatred of it, you automatically associate all kinds of negative things with it. However, it is possible to redirect the powerful emotion of hatred and then use the energy to do something positive about what you hate.

Through focusing on your life, taking a snapshot of it and then developing the negatives in your life, you would have a picture of the aspects of your life that you hate. You can redirect the powerful emotion of hatred and positively use it to change your life from worse to better.

If I have any advice to pass on, as a successful man,
it is this: If one wants to be successful, one must think;
one must think until it hurts.
(Roy Thomson)

DEVELOP THE NEGATIVES IN YOUR LIFE INTO A POSITIVE PICTURE

Do not despair when you focus on the negatives in your life.
You are in control and can develop them into a positive picture
and a remarkable success story. You would move from pain to
gain through constructively and positively redirecting your
emotion of hatred to tackle failure and problems in your life.
(Innocent Izamoje)

I have a lovely photograph of mine that was taken when I was only three months old. My extended family's culture – and the culture of many other families also – was to take a 'topless' photograph of their baby at the age of three months. The baby would be dressed up in lovely and padded underpants but without a shirt or blouse on. The baby's 'topless' chest would be beautifully decorated with a lovely necklace.

My 'baby picture' as I called mine was lovely. It showed me with a lovely smiley face and a potbelly.

For many years, I used the photograph to 'justify' why I could not slim down. I always believed and argued that I was born with a potbelly and could not do anything about it. You know the kinds of excuses people present when they do not want to go through the painful process of change; don't you?

A photograph of me at the age of three months offered me the perfect excuse I needed not to bother working out or using the gym or even doing anything whatsoever to slim down my potbelly. To make the matter worse, I really liked food. After all, I had a 'natural' potbelly and needed to fill it up!

My love for 'big food' continued from childhood to adulthood. Then one day, I developed my HOLD therapy; tested it on myself with regard to my eating habits and found that it really worked. I then taught the principle or therapy to other people who have reported to me that it worked for them also.

I use the principle in various areas. However, given that I am talking about food in this passage, I would cite an example of how I successfully managed to slim down my 'natural' potbelly by means of applying my Hate Or Love Discipline.

After carrying out a self-analysis of my eating habits, I realised that I ate a lot of food and retained a potbelly not because I was born with a potbelly but only because I loved eating a lot and hated a smaller portion of food. Therefore, I decided to hate a large portion of food and love a smaller portion instead. I did not decide to hate food because I knew the dangers of hating food; namely, that I would eventually stop eating altogether.

On the basis of my new decision regarding my eating habits, I hated a larger portion of food and hated my potbelly as well. Just by seeing my potbelly as disgusting and then hating it, I was determined to do something about it; and I did!

The day that I commenced the application of this principle with regard to reducing the size of my potbelly, I stayed in a 'Five Star' hotel because I was working away from home on that occasion. The company that I was doing the residential assignment for booked me into the great hotel.

The buffet dinner at the hotel was truly a 'Five Star' dinner with regard to both quantity and quality. I was seriously tempted to eat a lot. But because I had reformed my mind to *hate* eating too much, I deliberately only ate a 'One Star' kind of food at the 'Five Star' hotel. And I did this again and again and many times afterwards and then got used to eating a smaller amount of food.

My HOLD therapy works in any area of personal change: you can HOLD on to successful living by changing something through the application of the powerful emotions of love or hatred!

The problem with some people is that they wrongfully apply their love or hatred emotion. It is a real shame that some people love evil and hate good! I am not interested in a wasteful debate about what is 'good' or 'evil'. People who get real for whom this book is written know exactly what I am talking about. Give them a list of items containing things such as war, peace, child abuse, and decently doing voluntary work at an orphanage, and they would just know the ones that are good and the ones that are evil without engaging in a wasteful debate about what is good and what is evil.

The most important reason I used the powerful emotive word 'hate' at the 'body' or action level of my three-dimensional model of FAITH is because you would never succeed in life if you do not *hate failure*.

Most successful people do not say they love success or victory. Rather, they say they *hate* failure and defeat. If you only love success but do not hate failure as well, you would fail in some or many aspects of your life.

Sometime ago, I was concerned about the amount of coffee that I drank in a day. Therefore, I decided to switch from drinking coffee to drinking tea and in particular, peppermint tea. I love peppermint tea and some herbal teas. However, at the time, I noticed that although I drank the teas that I loved, I also drank coffee as well even though my reason for buying the various teas that I loved was to come off drinking coffee.

Just loving the teas that I loved was not sufficient to get me to achieve my goal of stopping drinking coffee. When I then *hated* coffee, I was able to stop drinking coffee. And whenever I had the temptation to drink coffee, I saw it as a curse and could not even touch it. The result of this personal experiment was great. Although I did not always drink the teas that I loved – for I drank hot or cold water most of the time – I always avoided coffee that I *hated*.

Even if you love success, you must hate failure also in order to really succeed and continue to succeed in life. When I say 'Love Or Hate Discipline' I am referring to deliberately hating failure or deliberately loving success through hating failure. If you do not hate failure, it would very much continue to be a part of your life in different ways. This is why you often hear **successful people say they *hate* failure rather than say they love success.**

I would like to cite another example to demonstrate how this principle works: Smoking. Many people have tried to give up smoking by looking at the pleasure that they could derive from not smoking. This is associated with the love emotion because love and pleasure go hand in hand.

Most people who look at the pleasure of not smoking and then stop smoking eventually start smoking again after a short period of time because, although they love the good health associated with not smoking, they have not consciously and deliberately *hated* smoking. However, when people decide to hate smoking and focus on the pain that smoking causes them, they quickly describe smoking as a dirty and disgusting habit and are able more easily and effectively to give up smoking.

People who really seek to hate smoking *do* things that help them to hate smoking including but not limited to the following things: they calculate how much money they spend – waste – on smoking and then note the pleasurable non-harmful things that they could put the money into instead; they note the opportunities that they lose as a result of smoking – something that is banned in many work places and public facilities; they visit hospitals to observe and talk to lung cancer patients who wished they never touched a cigarette in their lives; they note how smoking damages their health; and so on. The facts that they discover about smoking could enable them to hate smoking. They then constructively use their hatred emotion to give up smoking.

In order to avoid going 'up and down' in life, as well as loving 'X' things that you want, you must also hate 'Y' contrary things that you don't want. You must apply a holistic or full approach to love that includes both doing positive things and avoiding doing negative things.

In the context of this book, such a full approach to success means that you must love success but please hate failure as part of your love for success.

Loving a healthy life alone would not help you to give up smoking; you must hate smoking as well in order to give up smoking. If you were in a relationship with someone else, your love for your partner would not of itself necessarily and sufficiently guarantee that you would avoid having an affair with another person. Many people have an affair even though they really love their partners. You must hate having an affair in order to avoid it.

If you want another job but do not really hate your current job, you are not likely to seek actively to obtain a new job. If you want another car but do not hate your current car, you are less likely to actively change your current car. You might even buy another car whilst retaining your current car only because you did not really hate your current car.

Similarly, if you want a different or better situation in life but do not hate your current situation, you would not seek actively to change your current situation.

Naturally, people avoid what they really hate! You must be constructively and positively unhappy with failure, and then really strongly hate failure whilst obsessively loving success in order to guarantee your personal success in life.

Human beings are more effectively and powerfully driven by the impulse to stop something they hate than they are driven by the urge to start something they love.

Love and hatred are very powerful emotions. In order to guarantee your personal success in life, you must love success and use your love for success to open the front door of your life and move forward whilst constructively using your hatred emotion to lock and secure the back door so that you do not backslide into failure.

FAITH IS BABY-LIKE

Like the roaring lion on your hallway that approaches you without your invitation, problems come to people without invitations. People do not have to invite problems for problems to come to them. Some people compound their own difficulties by inviting additional problems. The result is that they get more problems!

Our natural state is a faith-based state. If you present the symbolic lion on the hallway to a baby, a baby would respond in a way that is significantly typical of a faith-driven response. If the baby could crawl, the baby is more likely to move towards the lion rather than move away from it; and if the symbolic lion opens its mouth, the baby is likely to smile – or open its own mouth also – because babies learn by imitation. The real point here is that a baby *has no perception of fear*.

In a serious sense, fear is not natural because we are not born with fear. Fear is something most people have acquired or learnt from various sources, including themselves.

The lack of a perception of fear explains why babies could play with fire. Even if a fire would burn them – and it does – a baby could play with fire because babies do not have a *perception* of fear or what I am really getting at in this passage: *a negative and self-limiting belief system*. In effect, I am not saying that we should not have a perception of fear – for fear serves a useful purpose of warning us of dangers. Rather, what I am saying is that we must not have *a negative and self-limiting belief system based on fear*.

Another issue associated with the point made in the preceding passage is that babies do not worry. Babies do not worry at all; unlike most adults who worry a lot and have sleepless nights over even little things that do not really matter in life.

Some adults are truly baby-like with regard to not worrying. They have successfully recreated themselves and they do not worry at all no matter what they face in life. They could be concerned about something, but they do not *worry* about it.

Therefore, another key thing that all adults must learn from babies is the construction of a faith approach to life. And we can do this through learning to 'grow down' just as we learnt to stop doing it as part of the process of 'growing up' in life.

YOU MUST CONSCIOUSLY CHANGE

Sometimes, people deceive themselves by saying things like: '*I can't change; this is me, I've been like this for years (or I've been like this since I was born)*'.

False. You have not been like '*this*' since you were born. Your mental make-up can and does change, just as your physical or physiological make-up can and does change also.

Everybody can change. People choose to change in the areas that they want to. When they do not want to change, they manufacture excuses that wrongfully present them as though they have always been like '*this*'.

To prove the point that everybody changes, just think back over the last year or two, or as far back as you can remember. If you get real with yourself, you must see at least one thing that you used to do – eat, drink, wear, say, think about, and so on – that you have changed in one way or another. Today, you no longer do it to exactly the same extent as before – it could now be to a greater or lesser extent – and today, you no longer do it in exactly the same way and manner as before or at exactly the same time as before.

When you get real with yourself, you really must find at least one way in which you have changed over the past years. This means that you have the capability to change. Therefore, you must constructively use the energy that enables you to change to make significant new changes in your life in line with the principles contained in this book.

EVERYONE HAS AN ATTITUDE

Everyone has an attitude. The real difference between people with a fear approach and those with a faith approach to life lies in their attitude.

Your attitude to life determines your altitude, your latitude and your longitude in life. The preceding statement is an unchangeable law of life regardless of your attitude towards it.

In the section following, I would give you some examples to illustrate the point.

YOUR ATTITUDE TO LIFE DETERMINES YOUR ALTITUDE IN LIFE.

I remember when my family and I first visited the Eiffel Tower in Paris, France. At the time, I was very fearful of the height of the tower. I thought I would feel sick looking down from the top of the tallest building in France.

Therefore, I used the long queue of people waiting to get to the top of the building as an excuse to 'justify' my not wanting to get to the top of the building. When we noticed that some people were actually walking up the tower, I used the fact that my left leg was previously fractured in a terrible road traffic accident as an excuse not to climb up the tower. Because of my attitude, I did not get to the top of the Eiffel Tower.

Your attitude determines whether or not you can stay on top of life and how high you could get in any area of life.

I would like to use another personal example to illustrate this point. When I was a teenager, I had an attitude that I would complete my university education and obtain my Ph.D by twenty-five years of age, get married at twenty-eight years of age, and so on. I have a video recording where I actually set out some of my life goals in front of my parents and other people during a social event several years before I achieved the various goals.

I completed my Ph.D studies when I was twenty-six years old having adjusted my goal as a result of a terrible road traffic accident reported elsewhere in this book in which I sustained multiple injuries; got married at twenty-eight years old as previously planned when I was a teenager and many years before I met my wife; and so on. Like many other people, I achieved various goals that I set for myself as a teenager because I had 'an attitude' aimed at achieving my goals.

The huge amount of literature that I have read about various successful people and the successful people that I have personally spoken to demonstrate that **successful people actually succeed because they have an attitude to succeed**.

Many people have been known to say, even at a very young age, what they wanted to become in life and they eventually became what they had previously visualised.

As a young girl at school, Agnes Gonxha Bojaxhiu who was born in Albania knew she wanted to work among the poor people in India. When she was only nineteen years old, she took forward her earlier vision and then joined a convent in Calcutta. After teaching for twenty years, in line with her vision, she then lived and worked amongst the poor and was eventually known not just to Calcutta but also to the whole world as Mother Teresa.

Take another example from India. As a young child, Indira Gandhi had an attitude to succeed in politics and she did. At the young age of thirteen, she took forward her earlier vision and organised a children's section of India's Congress Party. She later also took her childhood attitude to succeed in politics forward and eventually became India's first woman Prime Minister.

Having carefully studied the literature on the lives of successful people as well as having personally spoken to many successful people in various areas of life, I am able to say with great confidence that people succeed in getting to very high altitudes in various areas of life – as adults or children – where they have an *attitude* to succeed

YOUR ATTITUDE TO LIFE DETERMINES YOUR LATITUDE IN LIFE.

According to the Collins English Dictionary and Thesaurus, the word 'latitude' means "scope for freedom of action, thought, etc; freedom from restriction".

If you carefully analyse the definition of 'latitude', you should find that latitude is not just something controlled by forces or people external to you, but also by yourself.

Yes, other people or circumstances might restrict your scope for freedom of action and so on; but so can *you* if you personally have the wrong attitude. On the other hand, an attitude to succeed in life can enable you to overcome the restrictions imposed on you by various forces.

You should note that the definition of the word 'latitude' includes 'freedom of thought'. Whereas other people can control your "scope for freedom of action" or "freedom from restriction", nobody other than *you* can control your 'FREEDOM OF THOUGHT'.

A fascinating and challenging example to illustrate the point in this passage is the story of Helen Keller. When she was only nineteen months old, she became ill with scarlet fever and eventually became blind and deaf. As you would imagine, her only contact with the rest of the world was by means of touch. But she was in contact with herself, and in consequence, with the rest of the world, through her attitude to succeed.

Helen Keller's conditions could clearly have severely limited her latitude in life, but they did not because of her more superior attitude to life. She eventually learned to read and speak. She wrote books and articles, toured and delivered lectures all over the United States of America and Europe. And she succeeded because she had an attitude to succeed that determined, enlarged and enriched her latitude in life. Evidently, there are many other 'Helen Kellers' in this world who have used their right attitude to determine, enlarge and enrich their latitude in life.

YOUR ATTITUDE TO LIFE DETERMINES YOUR LONGITUDE IN LIFE.

Longitude relates to length. The longitudinal dimension of any aspect of our lives relates to extending that aspect lengthways.

As well as applying to various aspects of our lives, this point also applies to how long we can successfully live life. For example, if you have the wrong attitude to unduly shorten your own life and die within the next hour and then actively work towards achieving that unworthy and misguided 'goal', you could die in the next hour. Please don't embark on such a foolish mission!

When you complete studying this book and through the proper and diligent application of what the book teaches you about getting on and succeeding in life, you should be persuaded that life is really worth living and enjoying.

If you have an attitude that you want to live long, your right attitude would make you do things to live long; for example, how you look after your mind, physical body, the kind of food you eat and the extent to which you eat, the physical risks you take, and so on.

It's good to have an attitude. If you want something to last long – your life, your car, your marriage, your property, your shoe, your teeth, in fact, anything – just have an attitude to look after it and it would last long for you.

> *Successful living is not like Chinese food: Sweet-and-sour. Life should be sweet only and never sour.*
>
> *Unlike other living things on the planet Earth, only human beings have the godlike power to control and determine their own destinies by choosing the ingredients that make up their own lives.*
>
> *Therefore, you should choose only the things that would sweeten your life and the lives of other people around you.*
> (Innocent Izamoje)

CHANGE YOUR WAY OF LIFE

> *For the most part, fear is nothing but an illusion. When you share it with someone else, it tends to disappear.*
> (Marilyn C. Barrick)

A crucial way to tackle a fear approach to life is to identify and write down the things that you fear and then take specific steps to tackle them head on.

I invite you to carry out the exercise in the next section. After doing the exercise, come back to it when you have more time and are on your own in a quiet place, preferably in your own home. Ensure that you avoid any form of distraction when carrying out the exercise.

Exercise: Tackling Fear

- Write down the various things that YOU fear; for example: seeking help, taking reasonable risks, setting goals, going for a driving test, applying for a job, getting married, having children, travelling by aeroplane, and so on. Produce YOUR OWN LIST.
- Highlight the areas that would be easier for you to change right now. Concentrate on those areas. When you sort out the areas highlighted, your success story would empower and assist you to deal with the other areas.
- Have the hope that you would overcome your fear. Keep affirming the following statement to yourself until you feel that

you have personally owned it: '*I am overcoming my fears*'.
Remember: People acquire fear through learning and you can
also learn to stop fearing.

- Reform your mind to believe that you can overcome your fears
for you can. Just believe that you can and would overcome fear.
Think of any fear or problem you previously had that you
successfully overcame. It does not matter if it is only one small
example. Every journey starts with only one step. If you *think*
that you have never resolved a previous problem or fear, do not
despair; there is always a beginning in everything. I emphasised
the word *think* in the preceding sentence because most people
have overcome many problems or fears but *think* that they
haven't perhaps because they do not regard their success as a
major success story. **There is no hierarchy regarding
success. All successes are success stories**.
- Write down the specific things you can and should do to tackle
your fears head on **including acting as though the fear does
not exist**. Keep acting as if the fear is not real because, in most
cases, that is exactly what *FEAR* means: **F**alse **E**vidence (or
Expectation) **A**ppearing **R**eal.
- Strongly visualise yourself as succeeding in whatever you want
to do. Keep strongly visualising yourself as being guaranteed
success. Think of the wonderful things that you would do when
you succeed in achieving your goal. Through your mind's eye
see yourself doing them right now.
- Then strongly visualise yourself as taking the steps necessary to
achieve your goal. Keep strongly visualising yourself as taking
the steps.
- Then take the steps. And keep taking the steps until you
succeed in actually overcoming your fear as desired.

YESTERDAY'S UNCOMFORTABLE CHANGE IS TODAY'S COMFORTABLE HABIT

*Change is not made without inconvenience, even
from worse to better.*
(Samuel Johnson)

When we implement personal change in any area of our lives,
initially, the change feels uncomfortable. The principal reason
for the initial uncomfortability of change is because we are seeking to change from our 'old self' to our 'new self'.

People with a fear approach to life are so used to fearing that
it must initially be uncomfortable for them when they change

their approach to a faith approach to life. During the early stages of personal change, you would feel like a fish out of water. This is normal until at a later stage when you then get used to the change and your new circumstance becomes your new comfort zone.

As a result of a road accident reported elsewhere in this book, I could no longer walk immediately after the accident. I was on a bed in a hospital – lying on my back – for several months after the accident. Initially, it was very uncomfortable for me just lying on my back for several months without getting out of bed and walking about as I used to do before the accident.

Although, initially, I felt very uncomfortable just lying on my hospital bed, I eventually got used to it and no longer felt the physical and emotional pain of not being able to walk. Believe this: At about twenty-two years of age, I got used to being comfortable just lying on my back for several months and not walking! I didn't love my situation at the time for I wished I could walk again but it felt comfortable because I got used to it.

It was a terrifying experience the very first time I had to get out of my hospital bed. I loved to walk again but dreaded it because the nurses had told me that I had to learn how to walk again like a baby. And they were right. It was a fresh start indeed!

In the end, I was assisted to walk again and had to use some equipment to learn how to walk again. The transition process was painful and uncomfortable. At some points, I felt like giving up and going back to my previous comfort zone – lying on my back and just staying there. Now, I am very happy I decided to move forward rather than backwards.

When I started learning how to walk again – with assistance, of course – it was a painful and uncomfortable experience for me. Just lying on the hospital bed was significantly more comfortable than learning to walk again! In other words, my previous 'worse' situation – lying on the hospital bed – was significantly more comfortable than my new 'better' situation – walking freely again on my own two legs.

However, I knew that, as with every experience associated with personal change, I would eventually successfully go *through* the initial phase of uncomfortability and then get used to walking again. And I successfully walked again. Right now, it feels great doing the things – some of them to a lesser extent, for example, playing football, – which I used to do before the traffic accident.

The lesson from my own personal experience and from other people's success stories is straightforward: even where change is for better and definitely not for worse, initially, change always feels uncomfortable.

Your personal comfort zone might be to continue to live life with a fear approach or to accept failure or to settle to succeed in some areas of your life only rather than seeking actively to succeed in all areas of your life.

What most people do not know about change is that it comes in stages. Initially, it feels uncomfortable because it takes you away from your comfort zone. However, if you persist with change, you would get used to your new situation and it would then become your new comfort zone.

Today, I am walking again as a result of the application of the principle set out in this passage. I really felt comfortable lying on my back for several months after the accident reported in this passage only because I got used to doing so.

I could have chosen to remain in that comfort zone; but did not! Instead, I chose to go *through* the painful process of learning to walk again and being taught and assisted to walk again at twenty-two years of age.

Today, I am walking again even though I walk with a bit of a limp that, nonetheless, is significantly and qualitatively much better than permanently lying on my back in a hospital bed.

PROMOTING PERSONAL CHANGE

By asking you to recreate or refine yourself and adopt golden success qualities such as baby-like or childlike success characteristics, I am not saying that you should change everything about you. I am only asking you to get rid of aspects of you that do not promote your personal success as well as to seek to develop success qualities that would help you to move forward in life.

I invite you to carry out the following exercise with regard to the things that you already do and should preserve because they help you; things that you already do but should stop doing because they do not help you; and things that you currently don't do but should start doing because they would help you. In the section following, you should identify the things that you should:

Preserve – because they HELP you to succeed/remain successful.

Stop – because they DO NOT HELP you to succeed/remain successful.

Start – because they WOULD HELP you to succeed/remain successful.

Exercise: My Personal Change Programme:

Personalise the exercise by using the word 'ME'.

PRESERVE: Things that **HELP** *me* to succeed/remain successful.

1. ....

2. ....

3. ....

4. ....

5. ....

6. ....

STOP DOING: Things that **DO NOT HELP** *me* to succeed/remain successful.

1. ....

2. ....

3. ....

4. ....

5. ....

6. ....

START DOING: Things that **WOULD HELP** *me* to succeed/remain successful.

1. ....

2. ....

3. ....

4. ....

5. ....

6. ....

You could add more points to the spaces provided in the exercise.

LIFE COULD HAVE BEEN WORSE!

Believe this: Like every other person, your life could have been worse than it currently is! Honestly, your life could have been worse; and it might well be if you don't act *right now*!

No matter what you have gone through in life or what you are currently going through right now, things could have been worse. And they would be worse if you do not constructively change them.

I once met a middle-aged man on one of my management training courses. He was very calm, relaxed and seemed to take life very easy. He did not see any reason why people worry so much about life and live life as though everything in life were an emergency or a very big deal.

During our discussions at the training event, the man disclosed that he used to live life like most people. If most people want something they would not wait to have it because they behave as though they want it 'yesterday'. The man further reported that he used a major event in his life to change his approach to life: He suffered from a heart attack.

According to the man, although he did not like the heart attack and did not pray to suffer from another one, he attached his own 'good purpose' to the event and then used his own reason of why he had the heart attack to drive his life forward. On the basis of his story, I constructed an exercise entitled '*Life Could Have Been Worse*'!

I do the exercise with people on some of my personal and management development training courses. The exercise is quite simple but very powerful.

In my own case, whenever I have a strong urge to worry about something, I recall a road traffic accident and other incidents in which I clearly could have died. By simply recalling the events, they automatically motivationally give me something to be grateful to God and to other people for; and this then helps me to look more positively at my own life and to move forward.

The fact that you are still alive right now means that your life and your destiny are still in front of you. What you should be seeking actively and continuously to do is to move forward in life.

'*Life Could Have Been Worse*' is a very good motivational exercise. Whenever you feel that you cannot move forward in life, or whenever you feel low, just recall the major things that you have previously overcome and then note that *life could have been worse*! Then move forward so that life does not become worse actually.

> *If you look for something to be grateful for in life you will find it. I have found one for you: The fact that you are alive right now and reading this statement is something to be grateful for.*
> (Innocent Izamoje)

> *What we see depends mainly on what we look for.*
> (John Lubbock)

In the section following, I invite you to identify one or two crucial adverse things that have happened to you; or negative experiences that you have had that could have been worse.

They may have been very painful to you when they happened, or they may still be very painful to you right now; but your *life could have been worse*.

Someone you really loved may have very badly let you down; you might have been involved in an accident; you may have one form of disability or another; someone may have raped you; you may have lost your job, house or a loved one; you may have experienced 'this or that problem'; but you should remember one thing: *life could have been worse* than it currently is!

Exercise: Life Could Have Been Worse!

Identify one or two things that have happened to you in life that
could have been worse!

1. _____

2. _____

Well done.

**By identifying the things that you personally think could
have been worse in your life you are saying, at least indirectly,
that your life has really not reached the worst possible stage.
That is great! What you must do right now is stop your life
from getting to the worst possible stage**.

Everyone has something to be grateful for in life. No matter
how bad your life is or has been, things could have been worse!

Something happened in the preceding few minutes prior to
my writing this paragraph to test my belief in my own philosophy of life. I saw what happened as a test that I was determined
to pass; and that view enabled me to activate my philosophy
that things could have been worse.

Walter de Leon and Paul M. Jones were right: *"It's a funny old
world ..."*. It is indeed!

As I was writing the preceding passage, I was interrupted by
one of my sons who called me because he noticed that water
was dropping down from the ceiling into one of the rooms in
our house. I stopped my work to deal with it. Clearly, there was
a leak on our roof. It rained heavily over the last two days and
the storm damaged our roof. It was about nine o'clock at night
when my son called me to deal with the situation.

I immediately telephoned the emergency telephone number
of our building insurers to discuss the incident. They told me
that there was nothing they or anyone else could do to help me
in line with health and safety regulations because it was raining
and night-time. They advised me to telephone them again the
following morning.

I then did what I could do to temporarily minimise the
damage to our property until when the roof would be repaired
the next day. I told my family that there was really nothing else
we could do about the leaking roof, and that given that no
builder or roofer would sort it out for us at night the only other

thing we could do, was to pray that it would stop raining in order to stop further damage to our property.

We then prayed and I took comfort in the fact that it could have been worse. I recalled that some people's properties have been flooded in bad weather conditions but that the damage to ours was minimal compared to theirs. I also thought that the damage to our roof as a result of the bad weather conditions could have happened when we were on holiday and nobody would have noticed it for days or even weeks.

After praying that the rain should stop and having assured myself that it could have been worse – and I thank God it didn't get worse – I got back to my desk to continue writing this book.

As I write this paragraph, it's now about eleven o'clock at night and I have just looked out through the window and the rain has stopped. I thank God the rain has stopped; it really could have been worse!

Even when circumstances or problems evidently are beyond our control in life – such as whether or not it should start or stop raining – we can still DO something: pray about them; and then say 'yes' to whatever happens and accept it as part of life given that we have no control over them!

The real point being made here is that anyone who is alive can be a great success story and should be DOING something to promote their personal success in life.

I was impressed by the success story of Monday Emoghavwe – who won a gold medal at the Atlanta 1996 Paralympic Games – that was published in a recent edition of *Sports People International* magazine. He grew up in a developing country – Nigeria – where there are hardly any facilities for disabled people and was able personally to turn his own circumstances around on the basis of his belief that circumstances are not a barrier to living a fulfilled life. The short passage reported in the section following is an extract from his interesting and challenging story:

> *"The inability to use my legs … is a result of poliomyelitis, which I suffered at the age of 10. My parents were poor and could not give me adequate treatment. Even then, in the midst of my predicament, I lost my father when I needed him most. I was left with my poor mother … who took me to several healing homes, [but] unfortunately, I couldn't regain the strength to walk. Well, life must go on."*

"Well, life must go on" indeed. **For as long as you have life, you have the basis and the single most important requirement for succeeding in life**.

Whereas many disabled people have succeeded in various areas of life, most people who do not even have any form of disability present all kinds of excuses for failing to succeed in life; and whereas many people who had a troubled and painful upbringing have succeeded in various areas of life, people for whom everything seemed perfectly alright are unable to succeed in life simply because they fail to get real. *You* rather than your circumstances determine whether or not you succeed or fail in life.

My *'Life Could Have Been Worse'* exercise would also enable you to learn from past experiences and ensure that previous negative experiences are not repeated again and that the remnant or effects of previous negative experiences do not actually get worse. For example, if you lost your job, sustained an injury that could have been prevented, were badly let down by someone you trusted, made bad mistakes, or have had 'this or that' previous negative experience, just remember that *'life could have been worse'*; and then do things that would prevent the negative things happening to you again or that would ensure that your current situation does not actually get worse!

My *'Life Could Have Been Worse'* exercise also enables and then empowers you to look at situations positively rather than negatively. By looking at situations positively you automatically activate your personal power (of the mind) and then feel in control of the situation rather than seeing and then treating yourself as a powerless victim.

Remember: Like every other person, you would also encounter difficulties and problems in life; but the fact that you are alive to deal with the situations means that the situations have not reached their worst possible stage. Put yourself together and tackle the situations head on for *life could have been worse* indeed!

As you travel on the road to success, your task is to apply the breaks whenever things go wrong and then immediately stop them from getting worse.

PERCEIVE SUCCESS

Just know that you can succeed and you can!

There are times in life when we *just know* something that has not yet happened or has never previously happened or even something, which, on the face of it, looks truly very extraordinary and mysterious.

But how would you *just know* something? Some people describe the process of *just knowing* something as instinctive, some refer to it as gut feeling, some refer to it as self-confidence, some refer to it as telepathy, and others describe it as listening to the little voice that everyone has on the inside of them. Regardless of how you or other people choose to describe this extraordinary occurrence in life, people who get real in this world '*just know*' that they would succeed even before being engaged in an activity.

Many people spend their time and energy debating whether or not we can *just know* something. Other people, similarly, spend their time and energy analysing why we *just know* something and what the source of *just knowing* things is. Such an academic and theoretical exercise is of limited practical value.

The most important thing and the real thing that we should be interested in is that we *just know* certain things in life. Therefore, we should positively use information that we *just know* about. When you *just know* anything that would or could enable you to succeed in life, just get real and then get on with that piece of information.

Personally, I believe that God has a way of talking to us and that God talks to us even in our sleep – through our dreams – and also when we are awake by helping us to *just know* something. Our little voice that we have on the inside of us – a medium that I believe is a way through which God talks to us – can also warn us of dangers.

Several years ago, I parked my car on a road where I had previously safely parked it on very many occasions. On the particular occasion referred to in this passage, immediately I parked the car at the exact spot where I had safely parked it many times before, I *just knew* that something was not quite right with parking the car there on that occasion because I *perceived* that I should remove the car from that very spot.

Rather than get real and then listen to my own little voice, I suppressed it and reasoned academically that I had previously safely parked the car there – at exactly the same spot – without problems on very many occasions. I also noted that on the day referred to the road was as quiet as it had always previously been and that there was no reason for me to move my car away from the spot where I had always previously safely parked it. Therefore, I parked the car there as usual. However, something very unusual happened afterwards. When I got back to my car after sometime, I noticed that it had been very badly damaged. I then regretted that I did not work with the information that I *just knew* about before the incident.

I would like to cite a popular example to further illustrate the real point being made in this passage. You may have heard of the story of a little boy called David, who *perceived* or *just knew* that he would kill a big giant called Goliath even before his fight with Goliath. And he did. Because he *just knew* he would kill Goliath, little David had no fear; rather, he applied a faith approach and then achieved what he had *just known* would happen!

If you *just know* that something would or would not work, or that you would or would not succeed at something, just get real and trust your instinct or little voice or whatever else you use to describe the process of just knowing something.

The *just knowing* aspect of the real secret of success must be treated with due caution. I am not talking of circumstances where, because of fear, you *think* you just know you would not succeed at doing something; or circumstances where, because you do not get real, you commence a project on the basis of the misguided belief that you would succeed at it because you *think* you just know you would succeed at it.

The *just knowing* aspect of the real secret of success is like any other thing that you can hardly explain in any way – verbally, non-verbally, in writing, or in any other way – to another person without that other person directly personally experiencing it. If someone has never previously experienced falling in love, it is difficult to explain to him or her how it really feels to fall in love. Even if you try explaining it to them they could hardly truly understand you without personally experiencing it.

When you have your own direct personal experience of *just knowing* something, you really would appreciate what I am talking about.

Successful people have a very strong sense of perception. Like David who perceived that he would kill Goliath and then

did, they can *perceive* that they would succeed at something however difficult the things might seem.

Sometimes, you just know from previous evidence what the future is likely to be. At other times, you just know about something but cannot say exactly where it came from because there is no scientific and identifiable previous evidence or basis for it.

An idea could just flash through people's minds. Everyone has such an experience. While failures ignore such flashes, successful people grasp them, turn them into a dream, and then further turn them into reality through *doing*. It does not really matter if an idea crosses your mind when you are unconscious in your sleep; or when you are conscious and are driving on the motorway, eating, dancing, walking your dog, or doing something else.

When successful people *just know* that they can do something that truly seems impossible, they find a way to make it happen.

There is a beginning in everything. Therefore, you should accept that many of the great things in this world were based on ideas or information that came to people from 'nowhere' the first time they were made. Truly, people who perceived it from 'nowhere' invented many things that we enjoy today. They grasped an idea that they perceived or just knew about and successfully took it forward.

Everyone has the capacity to *just know* something and to successfully do something with what they just know about.

In order to succeed in life, you must have a very strong sense of perception and grasp ideas and information that come your way even if the ideas and information come to you from 'nowhere'.

9

THE *GROWTH* TECHNIQUE

Success in life is about 'doing'. The only nourishment that keeps your personal success alive is BREAD: Being Ready Everyday And Doing!

You will never succeed in life, let alone continuing to succeed, if you are allergic to BREAD.
(Innocent Izamoje)

It should be clear to you at this stage of studying this book that the only way to defeat failure in life – any area of life – is through getting real and then continuously succeeding. People who get real are doers.

As I have demonstrated in this book already, just as we 'grow up' we should also 'grow down' and be baby-like and childlike. As with 'growing up', 'growing down' is a language of success also.

The ideas regarding 'growing up' and 'growing down' do not refer to the biological process of ageing. They refer to obtaining and applying wisdom.

The application of wisdom is the principal thing that pulls together the other aspects of my *GROWTH* technique. It enables you to set *SMARTER* goals, analyse your reality, fully examine the opportunities and options available to you, identify and apply your talents, seek the right help you need, and so on.

'Growing down' does not mean 'moving backwards'. Rather, it means going back to basics and using the essential first principles of life *together with* other principles of success acquired in the process of 'growing up'.

It does not mean that X is wiser than Y just because X is older than Y. There are many foolish adults just as there are many wise children in all societies today.

Many adults physically 'grow up' without really properly *growing up* mentally, socially, and in other ways! And what they really need to do as they grow up is to apply the principle of growing down.

In the context of my *GROWTH* technique, the word 'growth' shows improvement, progress, flourishing, thriving, and so on.

GROW WITH THE FLOW OF CHANGE

Change is inevitable … . Change is constant.
(Benjamin Disraeli)

God, give us the serenity to accept what cannot be changed;
Give us the courage to change what should be changed;
Give us the wisdom to distinguish one from another.
(Reinhold Niebuhr)

Change is the only thing that is constant in life. Nobody can stop the process of change in life. Rather than attempt to stop the process of change that you can't, you would be well advised to grow with the flow of change.

There are things about us that we can change as well as things about us that we cannot change. I stated at the beginning of this book that we cannot change whether or not we are born or would die for everyone who gets in must get out; but that we can change and determine whether or not we GET ON.

My GROWTH technique is aimed at assisting you to *GET ON* by growing with the flow of success. 'Growth' is based on 'growing up' and 'growing down'.

To use a biological example, our growth and survival as human beings are promoted and sustained through feeding. In order for any living thing – our body cells, animals and plants – to experience growth or remain alive, that thing must be nourished. No living thing could survive let alone thrive without nourishment.

In order for success to remain 'alive' we must nourish it. The idea about nourishing success to keep it alive flashed through my mind one morning when I was having breakfast. As I picked up a slice of bread, I meditated on the fact that, as human beings, we need nourishment to be alive. Whilst still holding the slice of bread in my hand and meditating on how we nourish our body through feeding to remain alive, I just knew that we could keep our personal success alive if we nourish it.

Successful people are people with faith. However, *faith without works is dead*. I believe that my three-dimensional model of faith is truly excellent because it links faith at the level of HOPING – spirit – to the level of BELIEVING – soul – and then to the level of DOING – body.

Whilst still holding a slice of bread in my hand and meditating on the subject of nourishment in the morning referred to in this passage, I constructed the abbreviation BREAD that should serve as our *daily bread* for nourishing success and for keeping it alive in line with my growth strategy:

> **B**eing
> **R**eady
> **E**veryday
> **A**nd
> **D**oing.

'*Being ready*' refers to continuously putting on the clearly proven or ratified armour of success: getting real. And we must get real '*everyday*' and keep '*doing*' things that help us to succeed in life! 'Doing' is a present continuous word and it indicates that success is a journey. 'Doing' is not a one-off thing. We should continuously be doing things that continuously help us to succeed in life.

It is worth emphasising that **the only nourishment that keeps your personal success alive is *BREAD*: Being Ready Everyday And Doing! You will never succeed in life, let alone continuing to succeed, if you are allergic to BREAD.**

CHANGING YOUR LIFE AROUND

Shortly before writing this passage, I presented training courses for some organisations on issues associated with change management. I challenged the training course participants to turn things around in their own personal self-interest as well as in the interest of their organisations if they did not like the way in which things were going.

I engaged the course participants in carrying out a practical exercise which revealed that most of the course participants felt their organisations were merely surviving rather than thriving. We then worked together to point the organisations in the right direction: thriving!

As with the organisations referred to in the preceding paragraph, most people do not carry out a life-direction exercise to identify the direction in which they are going in life let alone personally taking helpful steps to turn things around if they do not like the direction in which they are going in life.

When I work with people on the subject of turning things around if they do not like the way that their life is going, I normally do what I call a *'Words Game'* to demonstrate my point. I offer people some examples and then engage them in a fun activity and get them to 'play with words' as a way of increasing their understanding of the change process and how we can turn things around.

> *Life must be understood backwards;*
> *But ... it must be lived forwards.*
> (Sören Kierkegaard)

Most people report that they are stressed. I challenge people who report that they are stressed to do something to positively turn their lives around. In order to demonstrate that a stressed life can be turned around, I get people to spell the word STRESSED backwards. It amazes people that when spelt backwards, the word STRESSED becomes DESSERTS.

Similarly, if you are personally living a bitterly STRESSED life, you can turn your bitter life into something as sweet as DESSERTS by turning around yourself, your circumstances and so on.

Another example that I use is the word STOPS. Many people report that 'this or that' problem or barrier stops them from making progress in life. I get people to spell the word STOPS backwards, and they then find that when spelt backwards, what they say STOPS them from moving forward becomes or represents SPOTS on the road to success.

When people get real, they find that they can *knock spots off*. The Ratified Evidence About Life has shown that a so-called problem that most people report as something that stops them from moving forward in life is a problem that they can tackle or outdo with ease when they get real. If it's *you* that personally stops you from moving forward, then you must *change your spots* or reform your character or mindset.

Another interesting example that I use with people when I get them to play my *'Words Game'* is the word 'NO'. I get people to spell 'NO' backwards to mean ON. If you think that there is NO way for you to succeed in life, you would definitely find a way and get ON when you get real! This observation is based on the Ratified Evidence About Life. People who get real in life get on!

An interesting example that I use to demonstrate how we can change our lives from worse to better is to see our lives as a puzzle. Our lives could be in pieces, but we can fix it by putting the various parts of the puzzle – our lives – together. As part of my *'Words Game'* I use the following letters: E, A, D, L. I ask people to see their lives as comprising of the various letters and then get them to fix it and turn it into something that makes positive sense. Some people fix the puzzle, that is, they turn their lives into the word DEAL and others fix it by turning the puzzle into the word LEAD. The lesson about this activity is to fix your life and to know that in order to LEAD a successful live, you must do a crucial DEAL with yourself: Get real!

As I stated at the beginning of this section, just as there are things in life that we can change, there are also things in life that we cannot change. I also use my *'Words Game'* to demonstrate this important and unchangeable law of life.

There are things that we should not bother to seek to turn around in life because we just cannot do anything about them; for example, the fact and law of life that everyone who gets into this world one day would definitely get out one day! I use the word DEED to illustrate this point. When spelt backwards, the word DEED remains exactly the same as DEED even if you *think* that you have turned it around. It just does not change.

According to the Collins English Dictionary and Thesaurus, the word 'deed' also means fact, reality and truth. The Ratified Evidence About Life has revealed that one of the facts or truths about life is that there are things in life that change and things that do not.

As part of my *'Words Game'* I also work with people to remove distasteful or unhelpful characteristics of their lives and to add to their personal lives qualities that would help them to move forward.

For example, if your life is reflected in any way by the word SWINE, you can remove the characteristics of your life represented by the letter 'S' in that word. If the letter 'S' is taken out of the word SWINE – your life – it becomes WINE. I believe that your life can be as sweet as the sweetest wine you can think of. Many people do not succeed in life because they have failed to remove the 'S' features of their lives. Many people still live with partners, stay in the company of friends, have wrong personal opinions and beliefs and so on, that prevent them from succeeding in life. In order to move forward and succeed in life, you must eliminate the 'S' distasteful characteristics and features of your life.

Similarly, you can and should take on additional characteristics and features that can help you to move forward and succeed in life. As part of my *'Words Game'* I get people to construct their personal goals and then add the other things that are necessary to achieve their goals. An example that I use for the purpose of this illustration is the word SEE. I work with people to SEE what they want in life and then remind them that when you add the letter 'K' to the word 'SEE' it becomes SEEK. Therefore, as well as having a goal, they also need to seek to achieve their goal. Remember: Seek and you will find.

Another interesting example that I use with people is designed to challenge people who feel low. Many people feel low, very low indeed! For all kinds of reasons, they feel inferior and physically and mentally depressed. I get them to think about the things they need to bring into their lives to turn it into a worthwhile life. When we add the letter 'G' to the word 'LOW' we turn our lives from LOW to GLOW. With a glowing life, we definitely have brilliance and an excellent feeling of well-being and satisfaction.

The crucial lessons associated with my *'Words Game'* are as follows:

- If you think that you are destined to fail in life or if you have always seen yourself as a failure in life, you can do a U-turn and move in the direction of success; for example turning a bitterly STRESSED life into a life as sweet as DESSERTS.

- You can find a way where you had previously thought that there was no way to move forward; for example, turning NO to ON.
- You can tackle and then eliminate barriers and obstacles that seem to prevent you from moving forward in life; for example, turning STOPS to SPOTS that you would then remove.
- You must accept that there are some things about life that nobody can change and therefore should not worry about changing them; for example the word DEED spelt backwards remains unchanged.
- You should note that life could sometimes feel like putting various pieces of a puzzle together and that rather than being puzzled about life, you should simply put it together in a sensible manner. For example, if your life is not sensibly and properly sorted out as in the letters E, A, D, L, you could sensibly put it together. The disorganised letters E, A, D, L, could sensibly be put together as LEAD and DEAL. This approach reminds you that in order to LEAD a successful life, you must personally do a DEAL with yourself by getting real. For example, when I got real with my personal happiness, I did a deal with myself and then drafted and signed in the presence of witnesses – my children – a personal happiness contract with myself.
- You should identify the distasteful characteristics of *you* that you must eliminate in order to succeed in life; for example removing the letter 'S' from the word *S*WINE in order to turn it into a better thing: WINE.
- You should carry out a self-analysis and then note the success characteristics that you do not have and must then develop and add to your life; for example taking on features represented by the letter 'K' that turns the word SEE into SEE*K*; or the letter 'G' that turns the word LOW into *G*LOW.

It is possible to live a glowing life. The GROWTH technique described in the section following would enable you to live a glowing life; and like the sun, you can shine and shine always.

I use the word *GROWTH* as an abbreviation. As explained in the section following, each letter of that word is an enabling letter of success. They enable and promote success.

G – **G**oals
R – **R**eality
O – **O**pportunities
W – **W**isdom
T – **T**alents
H – **H**elp

Everyone is engaged in the journey of life either as a *driver* or as a *passenger*. *Drivers* are in control and they drive their own lives forward. *Passengers* are not in control, and in consequence, are driven by circumstances and by other people in various directions. *Passengers* in the journey of life are all over the place; they do not know where they are going and are going nowhere actually. Everyone can and should be a *driver* in the journey of life.

Everyone is on the move in life. Some are moving forward or upward, some are moving backwards or downwards, some are moving sideways, and some are moving in a roundabout way.

You would find it useful to carry out the Life Direction exercise in the section following in order to determine the direction in which you are moving in life.

Exercise: Life Direction.

- In which direction are you moving in your life in general right now?
- Why do you think that you are moving in that direction? Specify as many reasons as you possibly can.
- Now, look at specific aspects of your life. Identify the key priority area of your life that you consider to be the top priority area that requires changing and improving right now; for example, schooling, professional work, voluntary work, marriage, friends, managing your time, money, spiritual development, leisure, personal development, and so on.
- In which direction are you moving in your top priority area right now?
- If you are not moving forward or upward in life with regard to your top priority area, what specific things should be done to ensure that you move upward or forward? By whom? When?

Begin to do your own bit today of what you require to move forward or upward in life and seek help from other sources including other people that could help you move forward or upward in life.

Thoroughly reflect on the preceding exercise. Check through your findings again. Then ask someone who is very close to you or a professional counsellor, mentor, or other helper who, objectively, could assist you, to work with you in assessing the direction in which you are going in life in general and in your top priority area.

When you have completed the life direction exercise with regard to your top priority area of change, you should go through the process again with regard to other areas of your life that need improving.

With regard to successfully implementing personal change, you should concentrate on your current top priority area. When you have ironed out your current top priority, you should then take on other bits one at a time.

Sorting out our lives is like doing a washing. Various things that have been messed up can be grouped together in the hope of removing the mess. But in order to successfully iron out various things in our lives, we must deal with each item one at a time!

My GROWTH strategy would assist you in driving your own life in the proper direction: forward or upward. Because success is a journey, my GROWTH strategy is based on a process. Growth is a process. We only stop growing when we die. Growth is a state of doing and it is boosted by our transition from human beings to human doings.

There are many dimensions of growth in life: physical, spiritual, financial, mental, and so on. For as long as we have life, we should continue to grow by doing things that boost and ensure our growth. Our realities change and we must address the changes; no matter how wise we are or how much we have learnt, there is always something to know; no matter how successful we are, we all still need help; and so on. Simply put, no matter how successful we are in life, we should continue to succeed by applying my GROWTH strategy.

In the Chapters following, I would deal with each element of the strategy.

G – GOALS

Dreams in life may seem impossible. They are not. Impossible dreams are achieved one goal at a time.
(Herman Cain)

In order to guide myself on the road to success I use a MAP: My Activated Plan.
(Innocent Izamoje)

In order to avoid leading a wandering life, everyone on the road to success needs and should personalise and then use his or her own MAP: My Activated Plan. I would assist you to construct your own MAP by showing you how to set doubled up SMARTER goals in a subsequent section of this Chapter.

Many human beings are like headless chickens! With regard to goal setting, the only real difference between a human being who does not have a goal and a headless chicken is that the human being has a visible head!

You may have heard the saying: *If you fail to plan, you plan to fail*. A crucial aspect of planning is about setting goals and planning how to achieve them. Successful people are clear about their goals and how to achieve them.

Unsuccessful people have something they – and they alone – think are goals; but on a closer examination, it would be clear that they do not have goals. Many people wrongly present their 'wish' or 'intention' as a goal.

A statement of intent, a wish or a vision has quality and value only when it is turned into a goal.

On one of my recent personal development training courses I asked the training course participants to specify their immediate personal goals. They verbally replied as follows: '*I want a job*', '*I want to go to university*', and so on.

I asked the group to think carefully about their goals again and then clearly write them down. The second time they did the exercise, there were two key improvements: they all wrote down their goals even though most of them simply wrote down what they previously said verbally and one of them reported that he wanted to go to university to study law rather than merely saying that he wanted to go to university.

Having an intention is having an idea. Ideas, like gold, must be refined to get maximum value. It is only when ideas become real goals that they have real practical value.

By setting *SMARTER* goals, you would be able to refine your ideas and turn them into valuable goals. In the section following I would teach you how to set *SMARTER* goals.

SMARTER GOAL

A *SMARTER* goal is a goal the various aspects of which are doubled up and reinforced as follows:

- S: Sound and Specific.
- M: Motivating and Measurable.
- A: Adaptable and Achievable.
- R: Realistic and Recorded.
- T: Tailor-made and Time–bound.
- E: Emphatic and Engaging.
- R: Reviewable and Rewarding.

The *starting point* for setting a real goal is to ensure that your goal is *sound*. The *finishing point* is to have a goal that is *rewarding* both to you and to other people. If your goal is not sound, it must NOT be refined for practical purposes even if it is specific, motivating, measurable, … and rewarding to you personally.

I would now analyse how we should set *SMARTER* goals.

Sound and Specific

Your goal should be sound and specific. A sound goal should be legal and ethical. Sound goals are based on a worthwhile idea or belief system.

There is no *right way* to do a *wrong thing* and there is no such thing as a *right thing* if it is done in a *wrong way*! The real thing in life is doing the RIGHT THING in the RIGHT WAY. The 'end' – *right thing* – and the 'means' – *right way* – must be justified.

I would like to cite some examples to illustrate this crucial point. Kindness is a right way to build and maintain interpersonal relationships. But you should not be kind to a child – *right way* – with the intention of deceiving and then abusing the child – *wrong thing*. Having your own shoes is a *right thing* to do but stealing someone else's shoes is a *wrong way* to have it.

If you still do not understand what *sound goals* mean, just get real and consider setting goals that you could proudly take into a television or radio station and broadcast to the whole world without being confronted by the police or real people who believe in setting and pursuing worthy goals.

When you have determined that your goal is a sound one, the next step is to make it specific.

Take this example by thirty-year old Sam – Samantha or Samuel: '*I want my own car that I would personally drive*'.

The statement above by Sam is a 'wish' or 'statement of intent' rather than a goal. However, if Sam has passed the first – soundness – test and has not been banned from driving and there is no other legal or ethical reason why Sam should not have and then drive his or her own car, the next stage in the practical process of turning his or her wish into a goal is to make the statement *specific* by refining it for practical and workable purposes.

To assist Sam in this process, he or she should go through appropriate steps from 'idea' to 'delivery' as set out in the example in the section following.

Idea: 'Sam wants his or her own car that he or she would personally drive'.

Given that this goal is sound because Sam has not been banned from driving and there are no other legal or ethical reasons why Sam should not buy and then drive his or her own car, the goal should then be made more specific as follows:

STEP 1:

Sam wants X type of car – specify type, model, age of car, and so on. Fully describe the kind of car *desired*.

STEP 2:

Sam wants X type of car by X time, the cost of which does not exceed X amount, and so on. Fully describe the factors – time, money, etc – that would influence or determine the purchase of the car. For example, when does Sam hope to buy the car, how much would the car cost, and so on.

STEP 3:

Sam is *doing* the following X things – such as saving X amount of money on a weekly or monthly basis – and in consequence, would be able to buy X car as *planned*.

Delivery: Sam has bought his or her own X car.

Congratulations, Sam!

In the example specified in this passage, I used three steps to illustrate the point. You don't have to use exactly three steps to make your goals specific. You might use two, three, four or more steps to refine your goal. What really matters is taking your vision or wish from 'idea' to 'delivery'. The number of steps depends on each person and how specific the intention that they start off with is presented.

Regardless of the number of steps that you apply to refining your goal, you must ensure that you get to the DOING stage. Remember: Success comes not from human beings but from human doings!

With reference to the example regarding Sam, you should note that Sam's *desire* was turned into an *action plan*. Sam's car was eventually successfully delivered not because Sam had a desire to buy a car, but because Sam turned his or her desire into a specific plan containing the things that he or she *did* to obtain the car.

Similarly, you cannot set a *goal* to be happy. Statements such as 'I want to be happy' are not goals. They are wishes and desires. You must turn your desire to be happy into a goal by identifying and then DOING specific things that actually make you happy. You would be happy not because you wish (or say that you want) to be happy but because you are doing specific things to be happy. The thing that you are *doing* is your goal that would enable you to fulfil your vision.

You achieve goals in life by *doing* things. You must DO things in order to move your vision, wish or desire from 'idea'

to 'delivery'. Therefore, goals must be refined and turned into doable action points.

Motivating and Measurable

It is crucial that you set goals that are motivating and measurable; something that is self-motivating and something that you can measure or know you are achieving or have achieved.

One of the helpful principles for success is 'BETTER AT' NOT 'BETTER THAN'. We are all 'better at' different things; no person is 'better than' the other. Many people fail in various areas of life not because they are not talented, but only because they are not good *at* what they are doing. They wastefully spend energy, time, money and other resources in doing something that they are not good *at*.

You must do or seek something that really motivates you. A motivating goal is an empowering goal; it empowers you to carry out your mission or to pursue your goal with strong will and determination.

Associated with doing or seeking something that is motivating, is doing or seeking something that is measurable.

In order to set measurable goals, you must clearly specify your goals in a manner that is practical rather than abstract. For example, you cannot measure 'happiness', but you can measure the sound and specific things that you should *do* to deliver happiness.

And as with Sam's example in the preceding section, when you 'conceive' happiness, your happiness would be delivered or achieved through the faithful and proper implementation of your action plan.

You must be able to measure the outcome(s) of your goal in some way. Some people and organisations refer to the yardsticks that they use for measuring their goals as *Performance Indicators*; that is, something that you can count, assess, or determine in some way that indicates to you that you are on track with regard to achieving your goal.

Depending on your goal, your measurable performance indicators might include any of the following examples: being promoted to X position in your organisation; gaining or losing X amount of weight at specific intervals or at the end of your 'weight gain' or 'weight loss' programme; being able to do X number of hours of voluntary work a week; being able to telephone X number of people to say hello to them on a weekly basis; being able to save X amount of money per month; and so on.

Adaptable and Achievable

Given that change is constant in life, your goal should be adaptable and flexible to reflect changes in your circumstance or reality.

I have adapted various personal goals in life. For example the 'time' I previously planned to complete my PhD studies was adapted after my involvement in a terrible road traffic accident reported elsewhere in this book. If I had not adapted my previous goal to suit my new reality after the accident, I would have considered myself to be a failure just because I did not complete my studies by the previously specified time. But by applying the adaptability principle to goal setting, my academic career became a success story.

Whilst many people do not adapt their previous goals, some people set goals that are not achievable. Arguably, although people can achieve all worthwhile or sound goals, YOU personally cannot achieve all worthwhile or sound goals. Because everyone has their own reality and talents, you must set goals that YOU personally can achieve. A goal to win the Olympics 100 metres gold medal is achievable, but not everyone can achieve that goal!

Achievable goals – in the areas in which you personally can achieve your goals – are better set as short-term motivating goals. To use the letters of the alphabet to illustrate the point, in order to move from 'A' to 'Z', you would find it more helpful to set a goal of moving from 'A' to 'B'. When you get to 'B', you should then set another goal of getting to 'C' and so on. As with learning to walk in life, you should take one step at a time. Such an approach and plan would help you to get to 'Z' as desired.

Achievement breeds achievement. Achievable goals are step-by-step goals. Even if you have a long-term goal, it is more helpful to break things down into smaller parts that are motivating and more easily achievable.

Realistic and Recorded

A realistic goal is a common-sense goal, a down-to-earth goal, a practical goal, a sensible goal, and a real goal for YOU rather than for other people.

Many people have goals that amount to a laugh because their goals are goals that *they* would never ever achieve. And they would never ever achieve such goals only because the goals are unrealistic when analysed from **their own perspective**. They set goals that are completely at odds with their past, current and future reality. As I write this passage, given the nature of my left leg that was very badly damaged in a road traffic accident it would be a big joke for me to set a goal of winning the Men's 100 Metres Olympics gold medal.

As well as not taking into account their own personal profile, circumstances and reality, people who set unrealistic goals do not also take into account the reality of the wider world in which they live. If you doubt the preceding statement, consider setting a personal goal such as filling up the Atlantic Ocean with sand!

Make no mistakes. Successful people do imaginative or crazy, but very realistic and worthwhile things. They do not do things that are silly, unreasonable, unrealistic, stupid, worthless and unnecessary.

It is sad, very sad indeed, that many people unrealistically live their lives in a manner that portrays them (symbolically speaking) as though they are personally sand-filling the Atlantic Ocean! You must be realistic in life.

A good goal has to be recorded. You should write down your goal for your own personal benefit. This serves to remind you of your goal and keeps you on track. People who get real know what I am talking about. They know that they do not write down practically everything they need or want to do in life such as having a glass of water or going to the toilet!

Organisations have adapted the vital principle of recording their vision. Many organisations have a written business or strategic plan. That is the point: strategic plan in line with their vision. By asking you to write down your goal, I am asking you to write down what you personally consider to be your strategic vision in life. You should write it down as a strategic goal or plan.

Remember: Real questions are the real answers to your real problems. **Personalise and then ask yourself the following crucial questions that would assist *you* in developing your own vision:** 'Why am *I* on earth'? 'What is the purpose of *my* being alive today'? 'What am *I* best at doing that would help *me* to improve my own life and this world'? 'Given that life is where everyone gets in and gets out but does not get on, what should *I* be doing in order to *get on*, and what would *I* like to be remembered for when *I* get out'?

Tailor-made and Time-bound

Everyone is a tailor. We consciously or unconsciously tailor our own destinies.

Similarly, everyone is a pilot. People often say that time flies. Realistically speaking, time doesn't fly; *you* do. Everyone properly or improperly pilots his or her own time and flies through life until we all eventually land at a place called grave.

An important message that I heard repeatedly as a child from my parents and teachers was this: *'Cut your coat according to your cloth'*. The message – which is assigned to J. Heywood – is simply to tailor-make your own goal for *you* in line with your own reality or circumstance. This is associated with being realistic.

Just as we all consciously or unconsciously do one thing – tailoring our destinies – we all have exactly the same amount of time to do it. Nobody has less or more time. Whereas people campaign, struggle and fight for equality, life has fairly given all of us a natural equal right with regard to time.

We are all equal before the clock. In life, there is absolute and transparent equality only with regard to time: Everyone has exactly the same twenty-four hours per day regardless of class, caste, marital status, age, race, sex, religion, and so on.

In many cases, when people think of the time wasted in their personal lives, they normally blame other people. After closely analysing how they spend their own time, they realise that their own self-management could seriously be at fault.

Successful people have a proper approach to assessing their own personal time management and they know how to avoid time wasters. For example, they effectively use the calendar, specify a date when they expect to start and complete a project, and so on.

Be adaptable as part of the application of time to goal setting. If you intend to get married, buy a car or start your university education by 'X' time just get real and change the – target – time to 'Y' time if your reality or circumstances change. Set reasonable timescales. The fact that Jack or Jill could achieve 'X' task by 'Y' time does not mean that Adam or Eve must work to exactly the same timescale. Everyone has his or her own reality. Know your own reality and work to it.

Emphatic and Engaging

An emphatic goal is a goal that is expressed and pursued with emphasis and determination. It is also a goal that is sharp or clear in form or outline.

When you set an emphatic goal, you should equally emphatically pursue your goal. In other words, an emphatic goal would engage your interest, your motivation, your attention and your talents. People commit only to a goal that fully engages them.

An emphatic goal does not contradict an adaptable goal. You should adapt your goal but emphatically stick to it. **An emphatic and engaging goal makes you act like a postage stamp: you stick to one thing until you get there**.

Emphatic and engaging goals are associated with *relevance* to you personally. A goal would not engage you and you would not emphatically pursue it if other people set the goal for you. There are many people who seek to get married by X age or to X person only because their parents want them to do so; some people study for a degree programme at university that they are definitely not interested in only because other people mentioned such programmes to them; some people do 'this or that thing' only to please other people or only because they are under pressure from other people to do 'this or that thing'.

Don't pursue a goal just because someone else has set the goal for you or just because you want to please another person. Your goals must be firmly placed in your own mind because you use your own mind to drive them forward. *You* **don't achieve goals in two minds.**

Reviewable and Rewarding

You must be able to evaluate and review your goal. You do not have to wait until the 'end' or until you achieve your goal before carrying out an evaluation or review. Some life goals such as goals that deliver happiness have no 'ending'; we must continuously do things (and review the things we do) that deliver happiness to us and to other people around us.

As you work towards your goal, you should regularly check progress towards achieving your goal, evaluate how well and how far you are going, and whether or not you are going according to your plan. The main purpose of your evaluation and review is to determine if you need to take any form of corrective action such as adapting or further refining your goal.

As I have stated already, 'rewarding' is the finishing point for a *SMARTER* goal. A rewarding goal is a beneficial and constructive goal that yields positive outcomes or rewards. You and the wider world in which you live would be rewarded as a result of the achievement of your personal goal or vision in life. Depending on your goal, the 'wider world' in this context could refer to one or two other people or a larger number of people.

Today we enjoy various things that were invented by various people who also got their own personal rewards from inventing them. When you do something beneficial in life, or when you set out to achieve a sound goal, you and other people would be duly rewarded even if, personally, you do not seek a reward.

I am not saying that you should *expect* a reward whenever you do something for yourself or for other people. What I am saying is that even if you don't expect it, you and other people *would be rewarded* in one way or another. **Sowing and reaping is a law of life and nobody can change it**.

When you do other people a favour, you 'sow' a seed, and would, therefore, 'reap' whether or not you personally expect a harvest or a reward. When I do voluntary work, it rewards other people and it rewards me also: I get a sense of fulfilment from it. When I buy other people gifts or donate money to a charity, it makes me feel good within myself; and this in turn rewards my soul!

Sometimes, without thinking about it, I might suddenly remember a circumstance many years ago in which I did someone a favour; and just the thought of it brings a refreshing feeling of joy to my mind.

If you want to become the chief executive officer of your company in order to expand the company and provide more jobs for other people and then personally receive a higher pay for your achievement, your goal would be rewarding both to you and to the world in which you live.

If your goal is to become the chief executive officer of your company in order to do criminal deals on the shares of your company and then run down the company; or if you intend to become the President of your country in order to cause a war; or if you intend to bring children into the world without providing or caring for them; you'd better get real and seriously rethink your misguided goal because it would not reward the world around you!

R – *REALITY*

People are always blaming their circumstances for what they are. I don't believe in circumstances. The people who get on in this world are the people who get up and look for the circumstances they want, and, if they can't find them, make them.
(George Bernard Shaw)

Understanding your reality is similar to looking at yourself in a mirror. You may or may not like what you see.

When you look in the mirror, the picture of yourself that you see could be lovely and pleasurable or it could be disgusting and painful. Regardless of the picture you see of yourself, you must DO something.

When you focus on your life, if the picture of your life that you see is fine, you must get real and continue to work at maintaining your personal success as part of successful living. If the picture of your life that you see requires improvement, then get real and take the steps necessary to improve your life.

For some people, confronting their own reality, in particular, their past reality and the remnant of their past reality, can be a very painful process. This is why some people actually break down and cry during counselling sessions or personal development programmes that bring them face-to-face with their reality. Your reality might be painful, but you must have to confront it and deal with it head on in order to get on and succeed in life.

And rather than stay in your past, you can turn around your past reality and the effects of your past reality into a glorious current and future reality.

The reality of a fish is water. A fish out of water is definitely in trouble. Just by looking at a fish out of water, you can tell that the fish would not survive let alone thrive.

Not all plants would experience growth in all circumstances. If you put various plants in their own 'reality' they would blossom. If you put plants that flourish in 'X' reality into a different 'Y' reality, they would not experience positive growth. They might not even grow at all!

If you put a fish on dry land or if you plant a tree in the wrong place, neither the fish nor the tree could change their reality because they do not have the ability and the godlike power of the mind to create their own reality. Therefore, they would not survive or thrive because of their circumstances.

But *you* are not like a fish out of water or a tree planted in the wrong place because you have the ability and the godlike power to change your own reality if you do not like it. You can and should create your own circumstances if you do not like the circumstances in which you find yourself.

CREATE YOUR OWN CIRCUMSTANCES

Unlike a fish or a tree whose growth or success is determined by the circumstances in which they find themselves and about which they cannot do anything whatsoever, you can create and determine your own circumstances or reality. If you do not like your 'habitat', you can and should create your own.

Understanding and analysing your reality would help you to identify the aspects of you that you must preserve and change.

On the face of it, it might seem that you should first examine your own reality before setting your goals. As with some people who have attended my personal development training courses, you might also ask why you should first set your goal before analysing your reality.

Some people have mentioned to me that they had previously thought that they should first analyse their reality before setting their goal because their reality should determine the kind of goal that they should set for themselves.

When I explain the way in which my GROWTH strategy works, people who previously thought that they should first analyse their realities before setting their goals change their minds and fully agree with me that it makes more sense first to set your goal before analysing your reality in line with my GROWTH strategy.

For the reasons set out in the sections following, you should first set your personal goal or goals before examining or analysing your reality.

Most people unduly limit themselves by wrongly looking at their situations first before setting a goal. If Helen Keller had first looked at her deafness and blindness before setting her goals in life, she would never ever have done the remarkable things that she did as a blind and deaf person; including writing books and articles, and giving lectures across Europe and America. Similarly, women who became Prime Ministers in a so-called 'man's world' and in countries where, evidently, there is sexism and sex discrimination, would never have set their goals if the first thing they did were to examine the reality of sex discrimination in the world in which they achieved their goals.

Most successful people in this world would never have set a challenging goal if the first thing they did were to analyse their reality or circumstance.

When you first analyse your reality or circumstance before setting your goal, you let your reality or circumstance determine your goal as well as control you. But if you first set your goal before analysing your reality or circumstance, you then determine and control your own reality or circumstance. If your reality does not help the achievement of your goal, you should seek to change it.

When you first set your goal before examining or analysing your reality, it would enable and empower you to do various things: set challenging personal goals; aim to put the 'extra' in ordinary things in order to turn them into extraordinary things; modify and adapt your goal as necessary; seek a different reality or even construct your own reality if your reality does not boost the achievement of your goal; and so forth.

Another key advantage of setting your goal before analysing your reality is that by so doing, it positively shapes your mind and enables you to avoid 'dead end analysis'; the situation whereby people misguidedly over-analyse things from a wrong perspective and eventually get stuck in a position where they cannot and would not move forward only because they *think* that they cannot move forward on the basis of the reality or circumstance in which they find themselves.

The real danger associated with 'dead end analysis' is that, by over-analysing things from a wrong and weak perspective, you tend to focus on your weaknesses rather than on your strengths; and you try and look for reasons that would stop you from moving forward; and because you would eventually find them, they then actually stop you from moving forward in life!

When you first set yourself a worthwhile goal on the basis of my *SMARTER* goal technique, you would find that when you then carry out an analysis of your reality, you would fix your reality to fit your goal including adapting your goal to reflect your reality; and you would focus on your positive sides and on how you would overcome the negative things that might stop you from achieving your goal.

Take the example of Tracey. She was interested in working but would never set herself any goal to find a job. In order to justify her lack of goal setting, she offered the following reasons – which I saw as mere excuses – for not setting a goal to find a job: her dyslexia, lack of formal academic qualification, and her inability to properly read and write.

Tracey was trapped in confusion. She had never previously worked and strongly believed that she would never get a job because of her personal circumstances or reality. Therefore, she never applied for a job and she never got one.

The fact of life is that if Tracey had set a goal to work, she would have triggered off her positive thinking mindset that would have enabled her to apply her creative mind to job search; and she would have found a job working for herself or for another person or in a partnership with another person or other people. In particular, even if Tracey were truly unemployable because no employer would employ her, she could have considered the option of self-employment or creating a job for herself.

When I first discussed with Tracey about job search it was clear to me that she had been unemployed for a long time simply because she limited herself. Her reality did not limit her.

You must understand this point. **People's circumstances do not limit them. People limit themselves by** *thinking* **that their circumstances limit them. And what they think about becomes real because it is real in its consequences**.

When, after a while, Tracey was able to set a goal to get a job, we then discussed the ways in which the barriers to her job search could be overcome. It was possible for her to focus her mind on getting a job, because, once she had set a goal to get a job, she was able to see her barriers as challenges. And she was able to meet the challenges head on.

After working together with Tracey on a career counselling and job coach programme, she eventually realised that there are many successful dyslexic people, and people who have various forms of learning disability as well as people without formal academic qualifications working either for various employers or for themselves; including some very 'big names' or celebrities she knew of. Tracey also eventually realised that she could create her own circumstances if the circumstances in which she found herself were unfavourable to her. Tracey is now happily employed and I was pleased to hear from her that she is doing very well indeed.

Analysing your reality means that you must fully understand yourself and your circumstances. In other words, you need an understanding of your own world and the wider world around you.

The analysis of your reality should be designed to promote your personal success rather than to hold you back.

You must be honest and very objective with yourself when you analyse your own reality. You must honestly and objectively reflect on the good and on the bad about you and your own circumstances. You must first see things as they are before constructing what you would like them to be.

The reason many people are unable to cope with various issues and, in consequence, fail where they would otherwise have succeeded is simply because they pursue things including very 'simple' things that are just beyond them; and the things are just beyond them only because what they seek does not reflect their own reality!

In order to succeed in life, you must apply a crucial principle of success: Understanding yourself and your circumstances and recreating yourself and your circumstances if you don't like them.

UNDERSTANDING YOUR OWN REALITY

When you have set a goal you should then objectively and honestly look at yourself and your own circumstances with regard to the things that would help you to achieve your goal as well as the things that might count against you.

Do not be put off by the list of the things that can count against you because in most cases, you can do something to change them; and in all cases, you can do something about *your response* to their effects on you.

In looking at the things that would promote or hinder the achievement of your goal, you should work very creatively and consider as many factors as possible including but not limited to the following areas:

Family:	What are your commitments? What are the kinds of help or barriers that you might face from your family?
Friends:	What are the kinds of help or barriers that you might face from your friends?
Other people:	Taking your goal into account, what are the kinds of help or barriers that you might face from your colleagues, competitors, mentors, sponsors, and other people?
Assets:	Do you have any assets that might help you?
The Law:	Would the achievement of your goal be promoted or hindered by the law?
Location:	Would your present location promote the achievement of your goal or would it hinder you?
Background:	How would your personal background or history affect your goal?
Money:	Is money an issue for you? Would it hinder or help you?
Time:	How much time do you need to allocate to achieving the goal in hand? How would this affect the time allocated to other activities?
Health:	Are you in good health? Has your health any effects on your goal?

The range of areas to consider would be dependent on YOU and your personal goal. Some people's current reality might include their professional work or career, schooling, and so on. Everybody has his or her own reality. In other words, everybody has their own various things that they need to consider as they seek to move forward in life.

HELPFUL AND RESTRAINING FACTORS

When you have identified the areas to consider, you should then examine the ways in which the things you have listed would help you or hinder you with regard to moving forward towards achieving your goal. In order to maximise the positive benefits of this activity you must carry it out with a particular goal in mind. By carrying out the activity with regard to a particular goal, you would be able to deal only with the issues that are relevant to the particular goal.

In carrying out the activity, you would find it helpful to do two columns on a sheet of paper using the style below to list the things that would help you or hinder you. Personalise the exercise by using words like 'me' or 'my'.

Exercise: Things that help me and things that hinder me

Goal: (Specify your personal goal) ...

Personalise this statement by owning the words "my", "me", and "I" in the statement: **With regard to *my* personal goal, *I* consider the following factors to be the things that would help *me* achieve *my* goal as well as the things that are the barriers that *I* need to overcome in order to move forward.**

THINGS THAT SUPPORT ME	THINGS THAT HOLD ME BACK
1.	1.
2.	2.
3.	3.
4.	4

You can add more points to the list above if necessary.

The objective of the exercise is to maximise the positive benefits of the things that would help you achieve your goal whilst eliminating or changing the things that would hinder you from achieving your goal; or at least, minimising their effects on you personally even if you cannot directly eliminate or change them.

Consider the following two questions:

1. How can *you* maximise the things that support you?
2. How can *you* eliminate or change the things that hold you back; or minimise their effects on you if you cannot eliminate or change them?

An important area that you should also consider as part of the analysis of your reality is this:

Yourself: The personal qualities that you have or do not have; including your experience, skills, qualification, beliefs, interests, confidence level, and so forth.

PERSONAL STRENGTHS AND WEAKNESSES

You should analyse your own personal strengths and weaknesses in the context of taking your particular goal forward. It is better to carry out this exercise with a specific goal in mind rather than merely doing an unfocused and untargeted list of your strengths and weaknesses.

When you have determined the specific goal that you would like to pursue, it is better to do two columns on a sheet of paper using the style below to set out your personal strengths and weaknesses.

Exercise: Personal Strengths and Weaknesses

Personal Strengths	Personal Weaknesses
1.	1.
2.	2.
3.	3.
4.	4.

As with the previous exercise regarding the factors that would help you achieve your goal or hinder you from taking your goal forward, your personal strengths are factors that favourably assist you in moving forward, whereas your personal weaknesses would hinder you from progressing or from moving forward in the way and manner or at the pace that you would have liked. Therefore, you should seek to maximise the use of your personal strengths and do something to overcome your personal weaknesses.

Consider the following two questions:

1. How can *you* maximise your personal strengths?
2. How can *you* eliminate or change your personal weaknesses; or minimise their effects on you if you cannot eliminate or change them (for example, a serious medical condition)?

CREATIVE THINKING

As well as being positive, potentiality, possibility, practicality, and permanency thinkers, successful people also think in a creative way rather than in a one-way or narrow way.

Some of the people that I interviewed as part of my research work prior to writing this book as well as those whose lives I have carefully studied visualise themselves as seeking advice from various individuals that they personally consider as worthy and successful in the area in which they seek to succeed. The visualisation process or method allows people to apply a creative thinking approach to an issue.

This method works in the following way: stay in a quiet place, make yourself feel relaxed and comfortable, and stay calm preferably with your eyes closed to avoid being distracted. Then visualise yourself as being in a boardroom meeting with key players in the field that you want to examine. Visualise yourself as having called them into a meeting to advise you. It's up to you who you personally pick to be in your mental 'boardroom' and the number of people you pick for the purpose of the visualisation exercise.

Whilst visualising everyone at your mental boardroom meeting, introduce yourself to the group and tell them that you would like to put an issue to them and then get them to advise you on the matter. Then present the issue to your mental advisers, focus on each person one at a time, and imagine what he or she is saying to you about the issue. Mentally actively listen to him or her and let them finish. Do not interrupt them. Then focus on the next person and do the same with everyone at your mental boardroom meeting.

When everyone has finished speaking, you should then mentally go round and ask each of your advisers if they have any other comments to make having listened to each other's views on the matter. If so, actively listen to their comments. By doing this, you would find that you are able to have various viewpoints on an issue. You should then group the comments that are similar together.

You would find it helpful to then write down your comments as the minutes of your mental boardroom meeting for further consideration before making a decision. Personally, I use pens of different colours in carrying out this activity; for example, green, red, black, and blue. I write down the issue that I want to examine at the top of a paper and then use the different pens to carefully write down different points associated with the issue as follows:

Green pen: Used to write down all the possible reasons why I should go ahead with an idea and the positive benefits of going ahead with the idea.

Red pen: Used to write down the negative disadvantages of the idea and all the possible reasons why I must stop taking the idea forward.

Black pen: Used to write down any threats associated with the idea and my personal weaknesses that might hinder me from taking the idea forward.

Blue pen: Used to write down the opportunities associated with the idea or issue and my personal strengths with regard to the idea.

CREATING YOUR OWN REALITY

You need to be creative when constructing your reality. What you 'see' is what you would create. You can see whatever you look for about your past, current or future reality.

When I run personal development training courses, I normally ask the training course participants to carry out an activity on personal visioning with regard to analysing their own reality. I do this in various ways.

For example, I do a colour exercise. My normal preference is to use the colours green and red. I call it *'The green and red colour exercise'*. To do the exercise, I normally write a 'Welcome Note' in green colour on a flipchart to welcome the training course participants to the event.

I ask the training course participants to look around the training room and identify as many things as they could find that have the colour red on them. I give them sufficient time to do the activity and tell them to mentally note everything in red or with the colour red on them.

I then ask the training course participants to close their eyes and tell me the things that they noticed in the training room in red or with the colour red on them. Everyone normally shouts out everything in red colour or things with a red colour on them.

Whilst their eyes are still closed, I then further ask the participants to tell me the things in the room in green or that have the colour green on them. Normally, most people are unable to say anything in the room in green colour or with the colour green on it and most people do not even remember the 'Welcome Note' in green colour on a flipchart that they saw prior to doing the exercise.

And even when I am wearing a green shirt or a green-coloured tie and have stood in front of the group for some time prior to doing the exercise, most people still do not remember the green on my shirt or tie or the green plants in most of the training rooms that we use.

At the end of the exercise we normally conclude that the participants remembered the red-coloured things only because they were determined to find them and actually went out of their way to look for the things in red or with red on them. People find the reds not because I tell them to but because they want to. Similarly, nobody and no book or programme can *make* you succeed; you succeed in life only when you want to!

Most people who carry out the exercise do not 'see' the green-coloured things. And the reason for this is not because there is nothing in green in the training room, but only because they were not looking for the green-coloured things. Therefore, even if they see a green-coloured thing – with their eyes – in the process of looking for a red-coloured thing, they do not remember the green-coloured things only because the green-coloured things were not seen by their *minds*.

In practice, what the exercise shows is simply that we do not see with our eyes. We see with our minds through our eyes just as we eat with our minds through our mouth. Your mouth would never eat any food that is distasteful to your mind.

Therefore, when you analyse your own reality, you should focus both on the obvious things that you might be attracted to look at and on other things that form a part of your reality and are relevant to the achievement of your goals.

Another exercise that I do with people that you might want to carry out is an exercise that is also designed to assist people in knowing how we all see things. I show people some letters of the alphabet and then ask them to write down what they saw.

Carry out the exercise in the section following and write down what you see.

Exercise: Creating Your Reality Through Personal Visioning

What do you see?

Activity 1: MYPERSONALSUCCESSISNOWHERE

Activity 2: AMISSISASTEPONTHEROADTOSUCCESS

Now, write down what you have seen.

Compare your answers with the following answers normally offered by other people:

Activity 1:

- 'I see a number of letters of the alphabet but can't figure out exactly what they mean'.
- 'MY PERSONAL SUCCESS IS NOWHERE'
- 'MY PERSONAL SUCCESS IS NOW HERE'

You are right whatever you saw.

If you saw only *a number of letters of the alphabet* you are right but would need to do more to sort out your reality. Although what you saw are a number of letters of the alphabet, you have to turn them into something meaningful, positive and helpful. Many successful people have turned their realities or circumstances that do not make sense into very worthwhile and helpful realities or circumstances that then enabled them to succeed.

If you saw *'my personal success is nowhere'* you are right. But you need to do more to sort out your own personal reality including your perception of life and success. If you look at your reality and then think that your personal success is nowhere, you should create or change your own reality to one that guarantees that your personal success is now here.

If you saw '*my personal success is now here*' you are right. You have a vision of success and believe that your personal success is right within your grasp. This positive mental frame would help you to construct a reality that would enable you to grasp what you see as within your reach. Having the right reality would help to guarantee that your personal success is now here.

Even if your reality were unhelpful, you should change it or create a different reality that enables you to actually grasp your success that is 'now here'.

I would now deal with Activity 2. Your responses to Activity 2 might be similar to the typical responses specified below.

Activity 2:

- 'I see a number of letters of the alphabet but can't figure out exactly what they mean'.
- 'AMISS IS A STEP ON THE ROAD TO SUCCESS'
- 'A MISS IS A STEP ON THE ROAD TO SUCCESS'

As with Activity 1, you are right whatever you saw.

If you saw only *a number of letters of the alphabet* you are right but would need to do more to sort out things including your own reality. As I stated with regard to Activity 1, successful people sort out their realities and turn them into sensible and helpful realities.

If you saw '*AMISS IS A STEP ON THE ROAD TO SUCCESS*' you are right only in the sense that it is a way of reading the letters of the alphabet clustered together in Activity 2. But what a way it is!

The Ratified Evidence About Life shows that amiss is definitely not a step on the road to success. The following alternative words for the word 'amiss' bears out this hard fact of life: awry, confused, defective, erroneous, improper, out of order, untoward, wrong, adrift, unsuitable, astray. Successful people don't go amiss!

You would definitely go amiss if you do not sort out your reality that influences how well and how far you can properly and suitably travel on the road to success.

If you saw '*A MISS IS A STEP ON THE ROAD TO SUCCESS*', then you have seen and are talking the language of success. This implies that you are focused and have a target in the first place, but that you might have missed your target or goal. That's not a problem.

Successful people adapt their goals and realities and try again and again and again. As part of analysing your reality, you should then adapt your goal to suit your reality or create a different reality in order to achieve a different result.

If you missed your goal, find out why you missed your goal and then fix your reality to fit in with your goal or fix your goal to fit in with your reality or DO whatever else is required – for example creating a different reality or goal – in order to ensure that your reality and goal blend with each other.

There is another point about missing a goal that is relevant to interpreting personal success. Although you may have missed your target or goal, you could well have been very successful indeed.

I once taught a class of students where Diana, one of my students set herself a target to score one hundred percent in a subject area. She missed her personal goal because she scored "only 95%" as she put it.

I believe that most people would not use the word 'only' to describe an excellent score of 95%. Although Diana stated that she 'failed' – not because she failed actually but only because she said that she scored "only 95%" – I believe most people in our real world would be happy with the excellent grade that she obtained in the subject.

If she had given her *very best* on the basis of her reality but achieved "only 95%" then it would be reasonable to take the view that she was truly successful and that her goal of achieving 100% might not have been a realistic goal in line with her reality as well as in line with the principle of setting a SMARTER goal. On the other hand, if, on the basis of her reality, she could have achieved 100% but only achieved 99%, then she would not be a true success story from her own perspective because she would not have given her *very best* taking into account her own reality.

If you miss a goal on the road to success, you should reflect on the goal in line with your reality and then take the action necessary to ensure that your goal and reality properly fit in with each other.

But if you go amiss, that clearly means that you are not going in the direction of success. If you go amiss, you are definitely going down a different road; and I truly mean *going down*!

Hopefully, the preceding activities in this passage would have helped you to see the positive side of things, a personal **quality** that you need when you analyse your reality in order to create a positive reality that would enable you to build on success.

I invite you to do a quick check on your willingness to seeing the positive sides of things by carrying out yet another activity. With regard to the activity in the section following, I invite you to look for the positive interpretation of the statement and write down only the positive thing that you can find or invent. Remember: Be creative and positive!

In order to further guide you in carrying out the exercise, I ask you to consider the importance of 'seeing' or personal visioning to success. I believe that you would agree with me that seeing or personal visioning is crucial to personal success.

Exercise: Creating Your Reality Through Personal Visioning

Look at the letters of the alphabet below and identify and then write down the positive statement or reality that you can see or create:

SEEINGISAWAY

Hopefully, you saw 'SEEING IS A WAY' rather than 'SEEING IS AWAY'.

Seeing or personal visioning is definitely a way to success. 'A way' and 'away' suggest movement. However, in the context of this book, while the phrase 'a way' suggests movement *towards* – success – the word 'away' suggests movement away *from* – success.

You should find a way to move towards success and not away from it! In order to find a way to succeed, you must be able to understand and honestly and objectively look at your own reality or circumstance. And you must look at your reality with a positive and creative mindset and then create a positive and helpful reality if your current reality does not offer you a way to succeed in life.

Regardless of what you are dealing with in life you definitely would find a way to succeed when you get real!

O – OPPORTUNITIES

… We must pick out what is good for us where we can find it.
(Pablo Picasso)

… As to luck, forget it. Luck is what happens when preparedness meets opportunity, and opportunity is there all the time.
(Earl Nightingale)

Make hay while the sun shines.
(English Proverb)

Just as the sun shines always, opportunities are always available to people. The sun shines always even if you think that the sun is not shining just because your part of the planet Earth has moved away from the sun. Similarly, opportunities are there always even if you think that there are no opportunities in life just because you have moved away from them.

Opportunities are available to people in various ways and people create opportunities in various ways.

However, rather than see an opportunity when it presents, most people 'see' other things such as disappointments, risks, and threats.

In order to succeed in life, we must maximise the opportunities that are available to us. Given that opportunity is there all the time, we must position ourselves to create opportunities that are tailored to our own needs and also maximise the opportunities created for us by other people and circumstances.

Many people have turned various things including a disappointment, a risk, a threat and even a tragedy into an opportunity;

and in consequence, into a remarkable success story. Before dealing with other related issues, I would like to deal with the issue of disappointments in relation to risk taking and turning threats into an opportunity.

A DISAPPOINTMENT OFFERS AN OPPORTUNITY

I see the word 'disappointment' as simply meaning 'this' appointment. In other words, the word 'disappointment' refers to the loss of a *known* 'appointment' or expectation. That is, a 'disappointment' refers to the loss of something in hand or something expected. Losing 'this' appointment does not mean losing 'that' other appointment also. In life, when 'this' door is closed, 'that' other door should be used to move forward.

The word 'opening' is an alternative word for the word 'opportunity'. As I have stated already, living life is a matter of making choices. When 'this' opening is closed, it does not mean that other openings are closed also.

A disappointment offers an opportunity for creative thinking. When other people disappoint *you*, they normally trigger off in you, the necessity to think about and then work towards having '*your own*'. Other people could unintentionally greatly bless you by disappointing you and you could create opportunities from disappointments.

A BLESSING MIGHT NOT BE A DISAPPOINTMENT BUT A DISAPPOINTMENT MIGHT BE A BLESSING.

I believe that you should agree with me that a blessing might not be a disappointment, but that a disappointment might be a blessing. In fact, a disappointment could be a very big blessing indeed. Something that comes to you as a disappointment is normally a blessing or an opportunity in disguise.

I know of a family who relied on someone else to offer then a lift home in his car each time they attended church. After enjoying a free ride home for a long time, the family was disappointed when, one day, the friend was, understandably, unable to drive them home as usual because of changes to his travelling arrangements.

Rather than moan about their 'disappointment', the family turned it into a challenge that they could meet. And they did! As a result of looking positively and creatively at their disappointment, the family worked towards buying their own car; and after a short while, they actually bought their own car.

I believe that if the friend, who on that occasion was unable to drive them home after the church service had not, understandably, 'disappointed' the family, they probably would not have thought of buying their own car, let alone actually buying their own car.

Whenever you face a disappointment, look for what is good or what could be good about it. Very often, a disappointment has an indirect positive advantage. As with other things in life, you would see the positive thing about a disappointment if you look for it.

I benefited greatly when I was highly disappointed by one organisation that I worked for.

I was appointed by the organisation to work as head of a training section. I had managerial responsibilities that enriched my job. Before I applied for the job, I had intended to set up and manage my own business. As part of my business strategy, I did not want to leave my job at the organisation until I had a good customer base with which to launch my own business. After some years in the training manager's job, I decided to work part-time in order to activate starting up my own training and consultancy business.

And although, eventually I had a good customer base to launch my own business, I lacked the drive to make the right decision to start off my own business at the time. In the context of my Hate Or Love Discipline – HOLD therapy – I *loved* having my own business but did not *hate* my job.

Therefore, I did my own business part-time and continued in the job until a day when I was extremely disappointed at what the organisation did to my job. What the organisation did to my job made me hate the job; and because I loved having my own business I was able to combine my love for managing my own business with my hatred for the job and then left the job.

Initially, I called what the organisation did to my job a disappointment. But when I changed my mindset and saw it as an opportunity, it greatly assisted me to start my own business on a full-time basis.

A disappointment and an opportunity mean exactly the same thing. The only real difference between the words 'disappointment' and 'opportunity' is the way in which the words are spelt.

The senior management team at the organisation where I worked as a training manager decided to re-structure many sections of the organisation including my training section as a result of which my managerial job was considerably devalued. This was both a serious disappointment and a risk to my professional development but I turned it into a serious challenge simply by seeing it as an opportunity. I did not change the situation; I only changed the way in which I saw it and the way in which I subsequently responded to it. My change of mindset greatly activated my desire to leave the organisation to manage my own business.

Now, I am most grateful to the organisation where I worked as a training manager for what they did to my job because, since I left the organisation, I have significantly advanced my professional and personal life.

As I write this passage, even if the organisation were to offer me my previous job back, and then double or triple or even quadruple the responsibilities and salary of the job, I would not accept the job back.

By devaluing my job, the organisation knocked my job but I did not let them knock my self-confidence or me.

One thing that I have learnt from carefully studying the lives of other successful people is to manage disappointments, risks or threats by turning them into positive energy through looking for what is good or what could be good about them.

Successful people believe that they could see what they want to see in any situation. Therefore, whenever they are faced with a disappointment or risk or threat, they look for what is good about the situation. They ask themselves relevant questions such as the following questions:

- Why did 'this' happen the way it did?
- What could *I* learn from the situation?
- What is good about the situation?

If they do not clearly see anything that is good about a situation, they would look for what *could be* good about the situation even if nothing seems good about it. They also seek help from other people who could offer them valuable insights into the situation from a different point of view.

As part of their analysis of a disappointment, risk or threat successful people also personalise and examine the following questions:

- How can *I* best use *my* time and energy to turn a disappointment, risk or threat into a blessing or an opportunity?
- What else could *I* do or see about the situation that might make *me* feel good rather than feel depressed or troubled about the situation?

A RISK OFFERS AN OPPORTUNITY

Just as some people could consciously be a blessing to you directly by offering you opportunities, so other people could, indirectly, bless you with opportunities by presenting you with situations that give the impression of being disappointing, risky or threatening.

As with a disappointment, you can positively look at a risk or threat and turn them into opportunities even though, unlike a disappointment, they might seem dangerous.

An opportunity and a risk are two sides of the same coin. If you look at a situation from one view, you would see it as a risk. If you see it as a risk, you would concentrate your mind on the dangers of the situation as well as on your personal limitations. You then feel weak and vulnerable and in consequence, would be unable to deal with the situation positively.

On the other hand, if you see a situation as an opportunity, the unknown would thrill you. You would concentrate on the positive sides of you and of the situation.

My initial desire the first time I was asked to address a national conference was to reject the offer because I thought it was risky. I feared facing a very large group of people. I was particularly concerned that as my audience comprised of people who themselves were training and personnel professionals they would unduly judge my presentation skills and would not forgive me if I made a mistake. However, I accepted the offer and changed my mindset to see the risk of doing the presentation as a golden business opportunity.

By seeing the event as an opportunity, I started focusing on the positive sides of the event. I reasoned that it would offer me an opportunity to advertise myself and my services, win businesses, raise my personal and professional profile, and so on.

Knowing that successful people do unusual things to achieve unusual results, on the day of the event, shortly before I was invited to the stage to – take a risk and – do my presentation, I went into the gentlemen's toilet, looked at myself in the mirror, and then said to myself whilst pointing at myself: '*Boy, you look cool and handsome. You can do it and it would be good*'! And I did the presentation and it was good indeed. Since that time, I have presented various other national and international events. I now see such events as an opportunity rather than as a risk.

Many people have been faced with various (more obvious and serious) risks that they turned into remarkable opportunities.

Clara Barton was interested in helping the victims of floods, famine, wars and other disasters. She took the risk of going as a volunteer to various battlefields to see what she could do to help wounded soldiers and other people. Her risk was a remarkable opportunity and she turned it into a success story. When she returned to the United States in 1874 after volunteering to help out in the war between France and Prussia during that time, she campaigned long and hard to set up an American Red Cross and eventually succeeded. She became the first president of the American Red Cross.

Benazir Bhutto turned a risk into a remarkable opportunity also. After military leaders in Pakistan who also imprisoned Benazir and other members of her family executed her father – a former prime minister of Pakistan – Benazir remarkably turned the risk that she faced into an opportunity to speak out against the military leaders. After her studies in the United States of America and the United Kingdom, she moved from a safe haven – places where she was safe, secure and out of the reach of the military leaders in her country of origin – and went back to a 'risky' Pakistan where she visualised an opportunity rather than a risk. She eventually successfully led her political party to victory and became Pakistan's first elected woman prime minister.

Successful people take reasonable risks. They know that it is risky not to take risks.

A THREAT OFFERS AN OPPORTUNITY

As with a risk, a threat offers an opportunity also.

Take the example of the corner shop businesses in the United Kingdom. In particular, from the 1980s, many corner shops emerged in the United Kingdom and they catered for a growing ethnic minority market. Most of the bigger supermarkets did not provide for the growing ethnic minority market. In consequence, the bigger supermarkets saw the convenient corner shops as a threat. However, they turned the threat into an opportunity. Today, many supermarkets provide various foods and products for ethnic minorities and have thereby increased their profitability.

During my last visit to Africa, a friend of mine stated that mosquitoes are a threat to life in Africa. I agreed with him but replied that mosquitoes offer opportunities also. Although mosquitoes are life threatening because they cause deadly diseases such as malaria, the existence of mosquitoes offer business opportunities to companies that produce mosquito nets, expensive malaria vaccines, insecticides, and medication.

Please don't get me wrong. I am not saying that mosquitoes are good. I am simply dealing with a fact regarding life as it is rather than, as it should be. Some people see mosquitoes as a threat and others see them as offering an opportunity. This is a fact of life.

As with mosquitoes, there are many other threats facing people in various societies today. By carefully analysing various threats in life, you could find an opportunity to do one thing or another about them. An opportunity to eliminate a threat is a great and wonderful opportunity and everyone should jump at it!

A TRAGEDY OFFERS AN OPPORTUNITY

Tragedies are unfortunate and painful. We wish we never had tragedies or disasters in life! Although it is unfortunate, a tragedy, like a threat, offers an opportunity also.

As I write this passage, one of the new legal developments in the United Kingdom is the implementation by the government of the Race Relations (Amendment) Act. The Act was part of the government's response to the recommendations of the Stephen Lawrence Inquiry.

Stephen Lawrence was killed in what was widely believed to be a racist attack. The Inquiry found that the police failed to deal with the murder effectively and pointed at what it described as the collective failure of organisations to tackle racial discrimination in the United Kingdom. Civil rights campaigners and the Lawrence family called for changes in the law and the government responded accordingly.

There have been similar developments in other countries. For example, the murder of a young girl in the United States of America led to what is popularly referred to as 'Megan's law'.

And the death of a child at the hands of a drunken driver, led to the establishment of Mothers Against Drunk Driving (MADD) an organisation that campaigns against drink driving. The unfortunate tragedies of families who lost their loved ones at the hands of drunken drivers offered an opportunity for various governments to toughen action against drunken drivers.

It is a shame that governments and some people have to wait for a disaster to happen before turning a tragedy into an opportunity. **The real opportunity offered by tragedies is the opportunity to prevent them from happening in the first place**!

Many tragedies can be prevented and everyone including individuals, governments and other agencies should learn from history as well as from possible tragedies; and then use the opportunities they offer to prevent future tragedies. You too should prevent tragedies in your own life!

A NEED OFFERS AN OPPORTUNITY

As with millions of other people, sometimes during the summer months, I suffer from hay fever.

Sometime ago, as part of my 'life review exercise' during which time I analyse specific aspects of me including my wellbeing over a specified period of time, I thought I should take steps to prevent the hay fever that I normally suffer from during the summer months. Therefore, I asked my medical doctor how hay fever could be prevented. He replied that hay fever is one of the odd medical conditions that can hardly be prevented. I believed him. However, when I put the same question to the pharmacist at my local chemist shop, he said something that indicated a vital opportunity for anyone out there who might be interested in the area.

Unlike the doctor who gave me what I described as a straightforward answer, the pharmacist replied that *'If anyone can do something to prevent hay fever they would make a fortune. That's an opportunity for you if you're interested in it'*. Although the pharmacist did not use the word 'need' in his reply, his response nevertheless indicates that NEED is a vital source of opportunities.

Just as millions of people have a *need* to prevent and effectively cure hay fever, various individuals, groups, communities and the world at large have a strong *need* for various things.

The various needs of various people present vital and various opportunities for everyone. A way to fulfil your own needs is to fulfil other people's needs.

If you have a need for a job, seek to meet the needs of employers who are looking for people to work for them. If you are thinking of working for yourself, do not look at your own need; rather, look at what other people around you need. Meet their needs and you would have created a job for yourself. In order to be loved, show love to other people for we all need love; and you would be loved because what goes around comes around. If you have a need to create wealth, simply look around you and you would see the things that other people need. Deal with the needs that other people have and you would automatically have taken care of your own need.

The above principle is a crucial law of life: give and it would be given unto you.

Given that people always have a need to be met, it follows that there are always opportunities in life – to meet the needs.

CREATE YOUR OWN OPPORTUNITIES

Associated with the point made in the preceding section with regard to meeting other people's needs, is the need to create your own unique opportunities.

We don't have to wait for opportunities to always come to us. We can and should create opportunities for ourselves. You can and should create an opportunity from a disappointment, a risk, a threat, needs that other people have, and so forth.

Opportunities are available or could become available to you through yourself, other people, and situations.

EXPERIENCE OFFERS
AN OPPORTUNITY

It should go without saying that our personal experiences as well as the experiences of other people offer us great opportunities.

Given that experience is not what happens to people but what we learn from what happens to people, successful people take time to analyse experiences in order to determine what they can learn from them.

You should analyse an experience regardless of whether or not it was a good or a bad experience. Many people have constructed projects and identified various opportunities from previous experiences – including their own personal experiences and the experiences of other people.

NETWORKING OFFERS
AN OPPORTUNITY

Nobody should live life as though he or she were an isolated island. Successful people are good 'networkers'. By networking with other people, you are bound to learn something from them – if you look for the opportunities that networking offers.

There are different kinds of networks: social groups, religious networks, network of friends, special interest groups where you network with other people with a common interest, political groups, professional or trade organisations, and so on.

Networking is not merely a business thing. In any area in which you seek to succeed, there is bound to be a way of networking formally or informally with another person or a group of people who can provide you with various opportunities for ideas, comfort, business, counselling, mutual support, and so forth. If such a networking group does not exist in your area, then you've got an opportunity to create one!

CHANGE OFFERS AN OPPORTUNITY

Change and new developments offer opportunities also.

For example, an organisation might be going through restructuring and change and many people could see this as an opportunity for a promotional move within the same organisation or elsewhere.

The birth of a child in a family is a form of change that offers the parents of the child opportunities to do things differently. The same applies to change when the child eventually leaves home.

Life is changing in various ways and there are new developments in life caused by us as well as by other people and situations. They all offer us opportunities for doing 'this' or 'that' thing!

EVERYTHING IN LIFE OFFERS AN OPPORTUNITY

Everything in life offers an opportunity. An opportunity is always there even if you don't personally see it!

People who get real create their own opportunities and maximise the opportunities that other people offer them. They do what I call environmental scanning: they scan their environments for opportunities and they fully utilise the opportunities available to them.

Exercise: Maximising Your Opportunities

- Identify the key opportunities that are available to you or could be available to you right now. (In identifying the opportunities that surround you, look at various areas including your work, contacts and networks, family and friends, community, and so forth.

  _____

  _____

- How can you increase your opportunities in life?

  _____

  _____

- How can you use your opportunities and turn them into tangible benefits?

  _____

  _____

W – WISDOM

*If you have built castles in the air, your work need
not be lost; that is where they should be. Now, put the
foundations under them.*
(Henry David Thoreau)

*People who get real have a burning desire for excellence because
they have plenty of wisdom. When you are on fire with
excellence and there is a lot of spark of excellence in you, your
success story would really spread like wild fire!*
(Innocent Izamoje)

**Success is unusual or uncommon. To achieve an unusual or
uncommon result you must do an unusual or uncommon
thing, including having your own unusual or uncommon way
of acquiring and applying wisdom.**

You may have heard the story of a man called Jonah who was
reported as having travelled in the belly of a fish for three days
from one town to another. On the face of it, most people would
argue that nobody could travel by such a means.

Whilst those who fail in life engage in such a wasteful debate as
to whether or not someone could travel below the surface of water
in the belly of a fish for three days, successful people who get real
acquire wisdom from such stories. Therefore, they construct their
own 'fish', give it a wonderful name such as 'X or Y Submarine'
and then use it to travel below the surface of water from one place
to another for three days or three months or longer!

When I was growing up as a young child in Nigeria, we used
to have twilight stories. Like most people of my age who grew

up in developing countries, my brothers, sisters and I did not grow up with things like television sets, mobile telephones, computer games and the Internet.

In most cases, we spent our after-dinner time listening to stories including folk tales that were designed not just to entertain, but more importantly, to impart wisdom. At the end of each story, we discussed the wisdom-based 'learning points' about the story.

People acquire wisdom from the university of life in various ways including learning from their own past experiences and the experiences of other people, listening to stories, watching wildlife, applying their creative minds to things, and from various other sources.

GETTING REAL OUTSHINES A PhD

Evidently, getting real in life outshines a PhD. The only way in which you can have a place in the sun and shine in life is to get real.

I know for sure that getting real in life is better, more valuable and more desirable than getting a PhD. I have both and know from my own personal experience what each one is worth!

You get a PhD from a formal academic institution. You get real from the university of life. A fish cannot learn to live in water and then live and thrive on dry land! You are simply a fish out of water if you think that you can live life and thrive simply on the basis of formal learning at an academic institution rather than through the application of wisdom acquired in life. We don't live in a formal academic institution; we live life. Some of the stuff you are taught at formal academic institutions are completely out of line with the life laws that govern and determine successful living.

A PhD is awarded to you following the completion of your studies after a specified period of time – about two to five years – that forms a very small proportion of your lifetime on earth; but getting real is a life-long thing and because success is a journey, you must always get real in life. In other words, a PhD symbolises your success 'yesterday'; a day that is gone and would never come back; but getting real symbolises your success 'today'. And TODAY is:

The
Only
Day
Available to
You.

Many people who don't have a PhD teach other people on PhD programmes. But nobody can ever teach you to get real if they do not get real themselves.

My mother once told me that having a *qualification* is not the same thing as having *education*. She added that the knowledge that you get from attending school is not the same thing as the wisdom that you get from the university of life. **We get qualifications at school but get education in life**. There are many highly qualified but uneducated people in the world today just as there are many educated people who do not have formal qualifications.

My mother did not formally study beyond primary school level. But she is one of the most educated, sensible and successful people I know. As I write this passage about sixteen years after completing my PhD studies, I know exactly what she meant when she compared the knowledge associated with formal schooling with the wisdom associated with the university of life.

I would like to use a driving example or illustration to make the real point here. You could go to a driving school and be taught driving. At the end of your schooling you could pass your driving test. If you pass your driving test, you would be given a driving licence that indicates that you have passed your driving test already; in other words, that you passed your driving test 'yesterday'.

Given that life is a journey and that we drive ourselves on the road to success, there is a crucial relevant similarity between successful driving and successful living. The real point about driving is not about passing the *driving test*; rather, it is about passing the *test of driving*.

Some people who have not passed a driving test and only have a provisional driving licence actually pass the test of driving and they successfully safely drive on the road. Yet, many people who passed a driving test 'yesterday' have been legally banned from driving 'today' just because they badly failed the test of driving today!

Real people know what I am talking about. Passing your driving test is a formal school-like thing conducted within a specified brief period during which time you might not face various challenges of driving including, but not limited to, road rage, someone driving towards you on the wrong side of the road – your own side of the road, burst tyre, possibly or actually dangerous mechanical fault, wet road, icy road especially driving on roads with black ice after a seriously adverse winter weather condition, someone jumping in front of your moving vehicle, and so on.

There are many drivers who pass a formal *driving test* but do not pass the *test of driving* in the university of life. Only people who acquire and then apply wisdom can be guaranteed to pass the *test of driving* their personal success programmes forward in life.

The real point being made here could be summarised as follows: A formal qualification is similar to passing a driving test. This is associated with measuring your intelligence especially in countries where people have to sit for an examination – the 'theory' aspect of the driving test. Successful living is like passing the test of driving. Only educated people who apply wisdom to life successfully pass the *test of driving* their personal success programmes forward in life.

GET YOUR OWN WARRANTY IN LIFE

Prior to writing this passage, this morning, when I was toasting bread, the toaster did not seem to be working very well. This triggered off a thought in me and I then reasoned that unlike human beings who do not come into this world with a manual, the toaster came with one. Therefore, I got the manual, read it and then started sorting out the problem with the toaster.

Whilst fixing the toaster, I considered the warranty that also came with it. Rather than continuing fixing the toaster, I started laughing because, just by holding the warranty in my hand, my mind told me an amusing but very serious and challenging thing about successful living: **Just as we do not come into this world with a manual we do not come with a warranty either. Life is the most valuable and necessary thing that we have that does not come with a manual or a warranty. Even a test tube baby does not come with a manual or a warranty!**

The only way you would have a warranty in life is to get real. Successful people who get real apply a lot of wisdom to life. Wisdom enables you to secure your own warranty in life.

WE ARE ALL LIFE LEARNERS

The most difficult challenges in this world are real life challenges and the university of life is the best place to learn about how to handle such challenges. By saying that getting real is better and more valuable than getting a PhD, I am not knocking formal academic institutions at all. I would not!

I have a PhD and studied at three good universities – the University of Lagos in Nigeria, the London School of Economics and the University of Sussex in the United Kingdom. I did my management trainers' qualification at a forth university – the University of North London – in the United Kingdom. Additionally, I have sponsored and supported other people financially and emotionally through their university education and have also taught at several universities.

Mark McCormack once wrote a book with a curious title: *What They Don't Teach You at Harvard Business School*. Harvard University is regarded by many people as one of America's top universities and as one of the best universities in the world. Yet, as the title of McCormack's book suggests, there are things that you are not taught and you do not learn at a university.

It is very sad that some people feel or are told that they are doomed to fail in life just because they have no formal qualification. Some people have been known to go back to school only because they believe or have been told by other people that the only way in which they can succeed in life is to have a number of formal qualifications. This is not true.

I am not saying that going to school or university is bad. I am only asking you to question your own MOTIVATION for seeking formal qualifications. If your motive for seeking formal qualifications is to guarantee that you would succeed in life or to learn how to succeed in life, then you'd better get real!

In fact, some of the things we learn at school are just not true and they are also counter-productive.

Regardless of whether or not you have a formal qualification, you can succeed in life if you get real. Don't put yourself down in life or let other people fool you by telling you that you would never succeed in life just because you do not have a string of formal qualifications. Whatever you do, just aim for excellence.

Excellence is the result of the application of wisdom. Excellence is the single most important way to overcome any barrier in life. People who get real have a burning desire for excellence because they have plenty of wisdom. When you are on fire with excellence and there is a lot of spark of excellence in you, your success story would really spread like wild fire!

The quality of your life will be determined by the depth of your commitment to excellence, no matter what your chosen field.
(VINCE LOMBARDI)

When you get real and apply wisdom to living life, you would understand what success really means. You would also understand that you could succeed and continue to succeed by continuing to get real.

Through using wisdom you would ask and then receive answers to wisdom-based winning questions that are relevant to your personal success programme. It is crucial that you find answers to your own questions rather than merely asking them.

WISDOM means: **W**inning **I**ncludes **S**uccessfully **D**eveloping **O**ne's **M**ind. In order to win or defeat failure in life and be a success story, as well as doing the other things contained in various parts of this book, you must also properly develop and then use your mind. Your mind is a powerhouse that generates wisdom which promotes success.

T – TALENTS

Know thyself
(Anonymous)

*You should positively develop your talents and creatively direct
your talents and other resources into areas of life where you are
'better at'. Every person is 'better at' something; no person is
'better than' another. Through focusing on areas of life where
you are 'better at' you would maximise your own personal
success with minimum effort.*
(Innocent Izamoje)

*There is a big difference between 'six' and 'half a dozen':
Six is shorter!
It is absolutely pointless using more words, energy, money,
time, or other resources on something where using less is just
as good. Successful people are not resource wasters.*
(Innocent Izamoje)

Unlike time – a resource that we all have in common and exactly to
the same extent – our individual talents are resources that uniquely
apply to each person. Everyone has his or her own talents.

**Success in any area of life is strongly associated with the
proper application of our individual talents and other
resources.**

Our understanding of our unique individual talents is
increased by the principle of **'better at' not 'better than'.**
Everyone is 'better at' different things; nobody is 'better than'
the other person. True!

People who apply wisdom to living life do not waste their time, energy and other resources in areas of life in which they would be struggling and then unnecessarily stress themselves out. Rather, they channel their time, energy and other resources to specific areas of life where they are 'better at'.

The principle of 'better at' enables and assists us to tailor-make our goals to suit our own reality and the areas of life in which each person is an expert.

By applying the principle of 'better at' you should be able to identify the areas of life in which you are particularly gifted and where you can personally succeed and achieve maximum result with minimum effort.

In order to assist you in identifying the areas where you are better at, you should consider the points set out in the section following.

Exercise: Identifying Your Unique Talents And Where You Are 'Better At'

- What do you really enjoy doing?
- What work do you do that you see as 'play' or a 'fun' activity?
- What would you want to do or prefer to do if you were able to pick and choose what you would like to do in this world?
- Think back to your childhood days. What did you really enjoy doing the most as a child? What did you enjoy doing as you were growing up?
- When you were a child, what did you say that you would like to do or become in life when you grow up? Ask your parents, guardians or carers to tell you the answer to this question if you cannot remember it.
- What have other people told you that you are particularly good at?
- In which areas of life have you excelled in the past? In which areas do you currently excel?
- What do you do that you do not *have* to do?
- Is there anything you really regret not doing and wished you could have done?
- If we were to ask people who really know you very well to specify the areas of life that you are particularly skilled or good at, what would they say?
- What comes naturally to you and in which areas of life can you maximise your achievements without sweating blood?
- What activities do you do and never experience stress? (Remember: Feeling tired is not the same as feeling stressed).

With regard to the point made in the preceding passage about stress, I would like to emphasis that feeling tired is associated with your – physical – 'body' rather than with your soul or spirit.

When you do what you really enjoy doing, after some time, you might feel tired but you would never experience stress. On the other hand, even if you have just returned from a lovely holiday, or have just completed having a four-week break or rest, you might immediately feel stressed the first minute you begin doing what you do not enjoy doing.

Many people who do not enjoy their jobs have been known to complain about going to work on a Monday morning after enjoying a weekend break. And after struggling through their stressful working week, every Friday they go home saying '*Thank God it's Friday*'!

By asking and then answering the kinds of wisdom-based questions contained in the exercise on the identification of your own personal talents, you should be able to identify the areas of life where you are particularly gifted.

Because we are all 'better at' (doing different things) not 'better than' – each other – we all can and should excel in what we do. We all can and should be number one in our own individual worlds.

When we do things that we are better at doing, we would enjoy what we do – because we would be doing what we enjoy and are particularly skilled at. And we should succeed because we would be self-motivated to activate our personal success and fully commit our energy, and other resources to our personal success programme.

If you are sweating blood and working too hard at something as though you are banging your head against a brick wall, then you are not the right person for it. Do yourself and the people around you a special favour: Stop! And then identify what else you should be doing – where you are 'better at'.

Everyone should work hard; but if you find that you are working *too hard*, in particular, if you are working too hard and making little or no progress in an activity, then the activity is definitely not for you. You would be well advised to identify your '*trade*' and areas where you are particularly skilled.

Your personal task is to examine and analyse your own reality and circumstance, as well as what you are better at and then fix your own goal accordingly. The goal that the person next to you – or even your twin brother or sister – sets for himself or herself is not an issue for you because everybody has their own unique reality and talents.

With regard to our own personal talents, reality, and other aspects of my GROWTH technique, there is no such thing as identical twins. People are just different.

As I write this book, the President of the United States of America is regarded as the most powerful person in the world. Personally, I would never set a goal to become the President of the United States of America.

A goal to be the President of the United States of America is a sound and specific, motivating and measurable, adaptable and achievable, realistic and relevant, … goal; but it is a goal that, personally, I would not seek taking into account the areas of life in which I am 'better at'. I am not good at playing the game of politics.

Personally, if I were given the job of the President of the United States of America on a plate – thank you very much – I would not accept it. And the reason I would not accept the job is because I know for sure that I am not *'better at'* that job. And I would not want to deceive the American people and myself by doing something I am not 'better at'. The American people deserve someone *better at* leading America to do that worthy job.

Anyone who becomes the President of the United States of America is not 'better than' me. No way! The American President should be seen only as 'better at' being the President and I should be seen as 'better at' doing my own thing. You too are better at doing your own thing. But *you must know your own thing and then get real and do it.*

The 'better at' principle enables everyone to feel empowered and to learn from each other without putting down each other. The philosophy enables people to value and appreciate each other and to see each other as successful in various areas of life. It also helps people to avoid unhealthy rivalry and competition and enables each person to concentrate on being number one in their own world and excelling at the various things they personally do rather than wrongfully seeing themselves as being in a competition with every other person.

The fact that you are reading my book to learn something and promote your own success does not mean that I am 'better than' you. No way! I am not 'better than' you. Definitely not!

The fact that you are using my principles contained in this book to promote your personal success only means that I am 'better at' writing *this* particular book. I strongly believe that you are 'better at' doing something else; or 'better at' writing a different book or article if, like me, you are a writer also.

In order to succeed in life you must know 'your own thing'. You must identify your 'business' or the areas of life in which you have special talents.

When I work with individuals, I ask them to carry out an exercise to identify if the jobs that they do are jobs that they are 'better at' doing and really enjoy doing. You might find it helpful to carry out the exercise.

I invite you to do the following short exercise in order to find out if your current job is your fun activity and something you really enjoy doing. I do the exercise with people as part of a wider activity designed to help them in identifying work areas regarding which they are 'better at' and have a natural talent, gift or expertise.

Exercise: Fun Work

If you were given five million British pounds sterling or American dollars right now, would you continue to do your current job?

When I put the question above to people on training courses, I normally receive very interesting answers.

Some people have said that if the money is given to them on their way to work, they would just return home. Other people have even said that if they won a lottery jackpot at break time, they would not even go back to their office to clear their desk. And some people have also reported that if the money is given to them after work, they would not even bother phoning in the next day or writing a letter of resignation because they just would not remember to do so!

If you answered 'No' to the *'Fun Work'* question as most people normally do, then you are simply doing something you do not enthusiastically enjoy doing. In other words, your current job is not your real mission in life!

With regard to being childlike in order to succeed, you must note that children, who **enjoy** playing, play the more they have the time and other resources to play with. They do not stop playing just because they have played 'five million' times! You know what I mean, don't you?

Similarly, people who are engaged in an area of life where they have a special talent would not stop working just because you have given them five million pounds or dollars.

As with children who could vary their way of playing when they are offered more resources to play with, successful people do not stop playing or working; they continue working although they might vary their way of working. Successful people would never stop working even if you give them this or that amount of money. And the reason is simple: they *enjoy* what they do and do what they enjoy.

Successful people do not work for money. Money works for successful people. Successful people, who enjoy what they do and do what they enjoy, excel at their jobs and automatically attract money through excellence.

Everybody can excel in life by doing things where they are particularly gifted. One of the crucial components of the real secret of success is to know your mission and areas of life in which you are 'better at'.

The 'better at' principle applies to work and to all other areas of life where people enjoy what they do and do what they enjoy.

Successful parents who enjoy parenting never stop. Even when their children leave their homes, their children never leave their hearts.

People who are not 'better at' parenting or who *do not enjoy* parenting don't even wait for their children to leave home before showing that their children have left their hearts: They do not care for their children and could abandon them or dump them somewhere; even in a rubbish bin, as some so-called 'parents' have done!

You must get real with this point: Do what you are 'better at' doing and regarding which you are particularly talented.

Recently, my wife, children and I listened to an inspirational and motivational speech by someone on television. He delivered his speech in the 1970s. And about thirty years on, and regardless of his age, he is still doing what he is 'better at' doing.

It doesn't really matter what your mission in life is; what really matters is that *you* know your mission and do what you are 'better at' doing; providing your mission is *worthy*.

You must *know thyself*: Identify your own unique talents and then do what you enjoy and enjoy what you do!

AVOID LEADING A CRAP LIFE

We can lead a successful life by effectively using our personal resources. Simply put, our resources refer to our supply or source of aid or support and a means of *doing* something. Our individual resources include our unique talents.

Everyone has his or her own customised resources or talents. The way in which people customise and then use their individual resources would strictly determine the quality of their lives and whether or not they succeed or fail in life. As used in this passage, the word 'custom' refers to 'practice', 'usage', 'way', or 'manner'. Everyone has their own way or manner of using (or not using) their own resources. That is, everyone has customised their own resources to their own way of life.

In order to avoid leading a *CRAP* life, we must avoid poorly using our individual resources or talents that we have all individually personally customised to ourselves. I use the word *CRAP* as an abbreviation and it stands for:

> **C**ustomised
> **R**esources
> **A**pplied
> **P**oorly

Rather than successfully and excellently living life, many people are living a crap and very poor quality life.

As well as applying to individuals the principle set out above applies to organisations also. Every organisation has its own resources that it has customised to its own culture. The word 'culture' simply means the way of life of a people.

With regard to personal success, the word 'culture' means the way of life of a person. Everyone has his or her own way of life. Everyone has his or her own customised way of using – or not using – his or her own mind, talents, time and other resources.

The challenge facing us in life with regard to our unique individual talents is to successfully live life by maximising our individual talents and other resources. Only people who get real can do this and, in consequence, avoid leading a crap life.

15

H – *H*ELP

Clapping with the right hand only will not produce a noise.
(Malay Proverb)

We all need help. Behind every successful person there is a helper.

Athletes, parents, footballers, road sweepers, kings, queens, teachers, students, writers, you name them; we all need help to succeed! Only foolish people say they do not need help in order to succeed; and this partly explains why foolish people never succeed in life in the first place.

Most people have a misleading and narrow view of 'help' in the field of personal development. They narrowly see 'help' as 'counselling'. In other words, when you ask most people to seek help, they narrowly construct it as meaning asking them to seek counselling.

Counselling is only one of many ways of receiving help. Help should be aimed at assisting you in taking your personal success programme forward. Help could be obtained in various capacities including counselling, coaching, mentoring, advising, support systems, and so on.

Those who help other people to succeed in various areas of life are referred to by various names.

Athletes and other sportsmen and sportswomen receive help from coaches; learner drivers receive help from driving instructors; students are helped by teachers; children receive help from their parents or guardians; political leaders are helped by special advisers; people with personal issues receive help from counsellors; expectant mothers receive help from midwives; workers and unemployed people seek help from mentors; those in care homes receive help from carers; people in various networks receive help from self-help support and networking groups; people who are ill receive help from medical doctors; people whose cars break down receive help from car mechanics; charitable organisations receive help from donors; friends receive help from friends; and so on.

I use the word 'helper' in the context of this book to refer to people who help other people to succeed in various areas of life.

Help can be offered in various capacities. People help other people in a personal capacity as friends; people donate money and other personal items to charities in a personal capacity; medical doctors, nurses, and teachers help other people in a professional capacity; parents help their children in their capacity as parents; and so forth.

The Ratified Evidence About Life has demonstrated that everyone needs and must receive help in order to succeed in life.

Even God sought and still seeks help in doing things! Various accounts of creation report that in creating the world, God said 'let us' create things not 'let me' create things. Additionally, many people believe that God does things today through angels and other people who might offer you a helping hand or bless you in different ways.

The real issue with regard to the preceding comment is simply that if the supernatural sought help in *doing* something, then it is crucial that – mere – natural human beings must seek help in doing things also. We have every justification in this world to seek and accept help in doing things in life.

As I have stated already, only fools do not accept help that is in their own interest. I qualified the preceding statement by referring to help that is in our own interest because there are some people who might offer you 'help' to which is attached all kinds of dangerous, often hidden, strings. We must reject such a 'helping hand' that is actually designed to take-away from us rather than give to us.

There are three kinds of helpers with regard to the final beneficiaries of the helping process: the self-directed helpers, the other-directed helpers and the mutual or reciprocal helpers.

SELF-DIRECTED HELP

The 'self help' or the 'them' kind of help is the 'help' that finally benefits the person or people offering it. In other words, *they* 'help' us only to help *themselves*. I call the 'them' kind of help the **'self-directed help'** because it is directed at the person giving or offering the so-called 'help' rather than at the other person who, supposedly, is 'receiving' the help.

Although this form of 'help' is based on and directed at the self-interest of the 'helper', it is often subtly disguised and pre- sented as though it is in the interest of the other person receiv- ing the 'help'. However, when you accept the so-called help from the 'self-helpers', you eventually discover that they never had your personal interest at heart.

People who help themselves through you might come to you desperately offering to 'help' you; or if you approach them in the first place, they would abuse the trust that you had in them especially if they sense that you are vulnerable.

Recently, I was made an offer by a company that introduced themselves as a window company. They offered to help me with newly fitted windows on our property for free. Although I told the salesman who approached me that we had only recently fitted new windows shortly before he contacted me, he, never- theless, kept bombarding me with his free offers and even offered to re-fit our fine windows that were fitted shortly before his first telephone call to me.

Because the so-called free offer was presented in an aggressive way by a commercial – profit making – organisation rather than a voluntary charitable organisation, and because I had no need for the windows on offer and had made this clear to the sales- man, I decided to carefully look at the 'small print' or hidden dangers attached to the offer. Eventually, it became apparent to me that the company actually intended to help themselves to my finances rather than help me with the windows on our house. The salesman no longer telephoned me after I referred him to the 'small print' in his 'free' offer.

There are many such suspicious offers of help in the world today. Some are presented in an aggressive way, but others are more carefully and cleverly covered up.

As I have stated already, 'helpers' who only help themselves by using other people do not have to come to you; they might abuse or use you if you go to them for help. The painful story of a man I know personally illustrates this point.

The man worked in the same town with another man who was distantly related to him. His young daughter attended a

school in the town. When he was transferred to a faraway loca-
tion, he decided not to disrupt his daughter's schooling
arrangements. Therefore, he approached the other man for help;
and the other man accepted to accommodate his young daughter in his home during the school term in order to remove the
immediate pressure on the father with regard to urgently sorting out her schooling arrangements. Sadly, within a short period
of time, the other man impregnated the young vulnerable girl.

You must be careful in seeking or accepting help from everybody because the Ratified Evidence About Life has shown that
many people who offer to 'help' you have their own, often
hidden, agendas or plan.

OTHER-DIRECTED HELP

The other-directed help is the kind of help that truly benefits
other people as receivers of the help. It is help that is directed at
the interest of the receiver and might benefit the receiver only;
for example advice given to you or help given to you by people
who do not stand to benefit from it in any way.

Because we all need help to succeed in various areas of life, I
also refer to this form of help as the 'us help' because it is
directed at us as receivers of the help offered.

People who offer 'us help' do not seek in any way to benefit
from the help that they offer to us. They simply help us from
their hearts. As part of my research prior to writing this book, I
found many examples of people who help other people without
intending in any way to benefit from helping the other people.
An interesting example was the case of a mountaineer who was
reported on television as seeking to find a man who once helped
her when she was involved in an accident and fell down whilst
climbing a mountain. She was seeking to find the helper in
order to specially thank him.

According to the mountaineer, a man came to help her after
she fell down whilst climbing a mountain. She stated that the
man must have been a medical worker of some sort or someone
very familiar with first aid procedures because of the professional assistance and advice that he gave her. She also reported
that the man did not leave his contact details with her but that
she wanted to specially thank him whoever he was and wherever he might be. She said he used his own materials to offer her

first aid and that she just felt she needed to see him again to specially thank him. When I heard her story on television, it was
evident to me that the man definitely gave her help that did not
benefit him in any way. Like the man referred to in this passage,
there are many people with a heart of gold in various societies
today.

Although people who help us might not seek directly to benefit from helping us, they, nonetheless, might receive a sense of
satisfaction from helping us.

One evening, I was driving in my car with my wife and our two
children. As we were driving home, we noticed that a woman
carrying a baby in her arms suddenly ran across the road to catch
a bus that was at the bus stop at the time. As she approached the
bus, the bus driver drove off and she missed the bus.

Having noticed that she missed the bus, and having noticed
the expression of distress on the woman's face, I stopped my car
and asked her where she was going. She replied that she was
taking her baby to the hospital. Having agreed with my wife and
our children to offer the woman and her baby a lift, I then drove
them to the hospital.

Although there was really nothing in it for my family and I to
change our travelling arrangements in order to offer such a
helping hand to the woman, we eventually felt a sense of joy
from having helped her and her baby get to the hospital.

The genuine other-directed help – such as the examples cited
in this passage – is the help that you give to other people without expecting anything back in return. Just do it from your
heart; and although you do not expect anything back in return,
you would find that by offering such a helping hand to other
people, *you* – rather than the other person – would bring joy to
your own heart.

MUTUAL OR RECIPROCAL HELP

There is help that mutually benefits 'them' and 'us'. The 'them
and us' helpers in life have an open agenda. They help us and in
the process help themselves also; and both sides know the
arrangement to help each other and are happy with it. I call the
'them and us' kind of help the '**mutual or reciprocal help**'.

Various people refer to the 'them and us' form of help in various ways including the following ways: '*Help me, I help you*';

'Win-win'; 'We're together'; 'Give and take'; or 'Scratch my back, I scratch your back'.

The 'them and us' form of help could be arranged in various capacities including personal and professional capacities. Friends help each other, married people help each other, people in a network mutually help each other, and so on. In a professional sense, within many organisations, there is a lot of professional back scratching going on and people help each other with information and support and in other ways.

QUALITIES OF GOOD LIFE HELPERS

A poor or bad helper is worse than none at all!

Regardless of the area of life in which you need help, you must seek and accept help only from people who have certain critical success qualities. Such qualities have considerable influences on the success or failure of the helping process.

There are certain personal qualities that make someone a good and effective helper. These include the characteristics set out in the section following.

Excellent Interpersonal Skills.

Helpers must be personable people. They should have excellent interpersonal skills and a proven ability to manage and promote good interpersonal relationships.

Relevant Experience, Knowledge or Skills.

Helpers must have experience, knowledge or skills that are relevant to the discipline or area in which they offer help to other people. This does not mean that you must be in exactly the same situation as the person you are helping. For example, an unmarried person who gets real can offer advice to married people through the application of wisdom rather than through direct personal experience of marriage.

Good Role Modelling.

Helpers must have credibility and integrity and they must do what they say. People should help you to do what they do well, are able to do well or could do well. Helping someone is not about saying one thing to them whilst personally doing another thing yourself!

Interested In Helping Or Developing Other People.

Helpers should like people. They must have an interest in helping or developing other people.

A Sense Of Humour.

Most people who need help reject it when a sad and grumpy person offers it. Helping other people should be a fun activity. As well as doing what we enjoy and enjoying what we do including helping other people, we must also be *seen* to be doing what we enjoy and enjoying what we do.

Proper Approach To Work.

It is crucial that helpers have a proper approach to work; for example, maintaining discipline during meetings, maintaining their role as helpers, and so on.

Positive, Possibility, Practicality, Potentiality, and Permanency Thinking.

As well as being positive thinkers, you and your helpers must also be very practical and believe that it is possible for *you* to permanently succeed. Your personal success programme should be designed to help you move forward in life through maximising your potential and abilities.

Able To Influence People.

Helpers should have some form of influence and be able to assist you in moving forward by influencing you rather than by exercising power over you.

Relevant Communication Skills.

It is crucial that helpers are able to demonstrate good communication skills including active listening, empathy, and the ability to give you proper feedback.

Personal Commitment To Your Success Programme.

Helpers should be committed to the helping process and to your success programme.

Confidentiality.

In many areas of a helping relationship, it is crucial that confidentiality is maintained.

Respect For, And Sensitivity To, Your Needs.

Helpers should respect your needs and be sensitive to your feelings. As part of mutual respect, helpers should also respect your 'space'; in particular, they should not invade your personal or intimate space.

Warm And Caring.

Helpers should be empathic, warm and caring people.

Considerate And Self-sacrificing.

Should it become necessary, helpers should be prepared and able within reason to 'go out of their way' or to 'go the extra mile' to help you.

Trustworthy.

Helpers must be trustworthy and people that you can rely on.

The Right Attitude.

It is crucial that helpers have the right attitude. They should not put you down or think that they are 'better than' you just because you need help from them. It is crucial that helping other people is based on the principle of mutual respect as well as on the basis of a shared ownership of the means and performance of the helping process and relationship.

THE IMPORTANCE OF SEEKING A HELPING HAND

People such as Presidents and Prime Ministers exemplify the importance of seeking and receiving help. Unlike most people, they do not wait for a problem to arise before seeking a helping hand.

When a President or Prime Minister is elected, one of the first things they do is to surround themselves with a group of helpers. It does not matter what the helpers are called: political advisers, or special advisers, or what in British political life is now being referred to as 'Spin Doctors'. A recent *London Metro* newspaper article reported that the British Prime Minister *"Tony Blair has 27 special advisers working in his department. They are among a total of 82 special advisers used by the Government"*.

Like political leaders and other people in positions of authority, we should all do the right thing about seeking help: Seek help now and always and seek help in various areas. We do not have to wait until there is a problem before seeking help.

Some people might argue that there are some forms of help that are needed only after a problem had arisen. They might ask, for example, *'Why see a medical doctor if you are not ill?'* or *'Why see a counsellor if you have no personal problem?'*

Evidently, people with a problem need help; but people do not have to wait for a problem to arise before seeking help. As many people may know already, you might find it very valuable to see your doctor at a time when you do not have any medical problems to worry about at all. Such a precautionary visit to the doctor's surgery would enable you to take preventative steps to improve your health. Similarly, by seeing a counsellor before a personal problem arises, you might well prevent the problem from arising in the first place.

A friend of mine recently told me something that I considered to be a very purposeful form of seeking help. According to him, before he got married to his wife, they both arranged to spend some time with another – more senior – couple whose marriage they regarded as very successful. My friend and his wife wanted to learn directly from observing the other couple why their marriage was very successful.

I like the way my friend put it. He said that he and his wife sought help from the more senior couple by means of counselling; but that they thought it would be particularly helpful to also spend some time with the more senior couple to actually observe first hand how they lived happily together.

When I heard this very unusual story about people doing a form of 'apprenticeship' with a mentor before getting married, I thought it was truly fascinating. My friend and his wife did not wait to get married let alone waiting for a problem to arise in their marriage before seeking help.

The real point about the example set out in the preceding passage is that we should all seek help now not at a later stage. Remember: You must personally activate your own success today not tomorrow!

What you should do is to identify your own life helpers; that is, people who can help you in various areas of your life and then seek help from them. Some people might help you with regard to your professional career; some could help you with regard to your health; others could help you with regard to various areas of life. In other words, we don't have to seek help from one person only.

When you ask for and receive help, you must avoid the so-called 'help' offered by people who only seek to help themselves by pretending that they are helping you.

Exercise: Life Helpers

- What is your current priority goal?

  _____

  _____

  _____

- Identify the people or groups – including organisations – that can help you move forward towards achieving your goal.

  _____

  _____

  _____

- Identify the specific things that you expect other people or groups to do to help you. (Ensure that you approach them and ask them to help you).

_____

_____

_____

PUT YOUR HEART AND MINE TO IT.

In order to motivate other people to help you in life, you first have to put your own heart to your own personal success programme.

As any helper would tell you, if you do not put your own heart to your own personal success programme, it would be more difficult for your helper to actually help you or put their heart to your success programme. There is a shared ownership of the helping process and you must do your own bit and be seen by your helper to be doing your own bit. Your personal commitment to your own success programme is crucial because helpers more effectively help those who help themselves.

In my experience as a helper, I normally find it easier to work with people who are personally interested in moving forward in life. It does not really matter the problem they present. A crucial thing is their motivation, willingness and commitment to moving forward through demonstrably ensuring that their problem is resolved.

Just as other people help you to succeed so you should also help other people to succeed by helping them in the areas of life in which you are 'better at'.

The person who gives and the person who receives do exactly the same thing: they both stretch out their arms.

Remember to seek help and stretch forth your arm to receive it and someone out there would offer you a helping hand. Remember also that someone out there is stretching forth his or her arm to receive help and you might well be the person that could help him or her.

Real people know that what goes around on earth comes around. When you help other people, other people would help you too!

Billy Graham is right: the reason we come to this world with two hands is because one is for 'giving' and the other is for 'receiving'.

The hand that gives, gathers.
(English Proverb)

16

CONCLUSION:
A SPECIAL CASE

Life is like a cake. Various ingredients are required to put it together. You can make it the way you personally want it to be and you can make it as sweet as you wish. You enjoy it. And you share it with other people also.

I recently attended a wedding ceremony. As the celebration continued at the successful wedding event, it reminded me of life in general and the fact that life can and should be celebrated.

The couple at the wedding event did not eat their wedding cake on their own. They cut the cake and then ate it together with other people. They evidently enjoyed the cake and so did the other people around them. Similarly, we should succeed in life, enjoy our personal success and also be a blessing to the wider world in which we live. We can enjoy life and also promote other people's enjoyment of life by being a blessing to them in different ways.

Successful people celebrate success. They reward themselves and other people for their success.

Given that success is a journey, I asked separate groups of people on some of my recent self-management training courses to list the various ways in which they *regularly* reward themselves and other people as part of the process of celebrating success. The groups identified the following 'goodies':

- Travelling/going on holiday.
- Congratulating oneself.
- Thanksgiving – thanking God, oneself, and other people – helpers.
- Having a party.
- Having a drink.
- Buying new things – car, clothes, house, and so on.

- Making love.
- Eating out/giving oneself a fun food treat.
- Buying oneself and other people gifts.
- Making donations to charitable organisations.
- Going to watch an interesting live sporting event.
- Going to watch an interesting live comedy.
- Going to the Cinema/Theatre.
- Dancing.

The list in the preceding section is not designed to suggest the ways to celebrate success. Rather, it is only a report of the ways in which some people stated that they celebrate success. I am not suggesting that you should celebrate success in exactly the same ways. Different people celebrate success in different ways and it is up to each person to identify their own way of regularly celebrating success. It is very much up to you to do what you enjoy and enjoy what you do with regard to the celebration of success and in every other area of life. But one thing you must do is to celebrate success – in your own way!

It is important to note that your personal reward systems must reflect your own reality including things that you personally enjoy, things that you can afford, and so on. Given that success is a journey, you must have a system in place for regularly rewarding yourself and other people. For example, each successful step taken on the road to success is a success story in itself and duly justifies you to reward yourself.

In order to assist you in identifying the various ways in which you can and should reward yourself or other people for helping you to succeed in life, you should specify in the spaces in the section following, the reward systems that apply to your own personal reality. Be creative as you do this activity.

Exercise: Personal Reward Systems

My personal reward package includes the following 'goodies':

_____	_____	_____
_____	_____	_____
_____	_____	_____
_____	_____	_____
_____	_____	_____

Rewarding yourself is an integral aspect of the journey of success. In particular, whenever you complete a step or achieve something within a specified time limit, you need to reward yourself for your personal success.

And as part of caring for each other, ask your friends, family, mentors, mentees, and other people who are close to you to give you a reward when they see that you are doing or have done what you committed to do. On your part, you should also reward other people when you notice that they are doing or have done what they committed themselves to doing.

Rewarding yourself is not optional; it is part of the real secret of success. As well as patting yourself and other people on the back for attaining success, you can also use personal reward systems to motivate yourself and other people when you notice that you or other people are becoming discouraged. Rewards help you to refill and recharge your 'batteries'. Rewards motivate people to move forward and rewards help people to sharpen the saw with which they cut down barriers on the road to success.

As I stated at the beginning of this Chapter, life is like a cake. Just as various things are properly put together to make a lovely cake, so you must also properly put various things together in your life to make your life lovely and sweet.

A person who needs special attention is referred to as a 'case'. Every person is special and we all deserve special attention from ourselves.

The truth is out there.
(Chris Carter)

We dance round in a ring and suppose,
But the Secret sits in the middle and knows.
(Robert Frost)

The world is full of many secrets. You do not have to know all of them. However, there is one secret in this world that every person must know and apply *today*: the real secret of success.

Everyone who has ever lived did not know every secret in this world and you must never seek to know every secret in this world because you don't NEED to. You don't have a need to know when your neighbour down the road actually slept last night or how long he or she sleeps for. You don't need to know if they are sleeping right now or have woken up.

But you must take personal responsibility for your own wake up call in this world and wake yourself up and then activate your own journey on the road to success. You must remember that although everyone dreams, the only people who succeed in our real world are those who wake up and DO something about their dreams.

And when you wake up, you must also remember that failing to properly DO what you must do to succeed would turn your dream into a daydream or a frightening nightmare.

You must remember to dream big dreams and never be discouraged because every big or great thing in this world was once considered impossible. When you have a big dream and mention your dream to other people they might muck you or call you names. They might even think you are mad only because you have an unusual big dream. You are not the first person to be nicknamed a dreamer and you would never be the last.

Very many years ago, a young man called Joseph had big dreams. He dreamt of becoming the viceroy or Prime Minister of Egypt. People around him including members of his own family mucked him and called him a dreamer.

Joseph's brothers beat him up and eventually sold him as a slave. But 'Joseph the dreamer' was also 'Joseph the doer'. In line with his dream, he was 'lucky' only as a result of personally activating his own success through DOING things that eventually enabled him to become the viceroy or Prime Minister of Egypt.

And when Joseph's dream succeeded and he became the viceroy or Prime Minister of Egypt, he was a blessing not just to himself but also to other people including his own family that sold him as a slave. Like the couple at the wedding event referred to at the beginning of this Chapter, Joseph not only ate from his (symbolic) 'cake', but he also blessed other people with it.

Nelson Mandela's family did not sell him as a slave. But as a doer and as a real person, after spending about twenty-seven years slavishly in jail – during which time most people would have completely given up and abandoned their dream – Mandela was able to achieve his dream. And when he became President of South Africa he was a true blessing to the world at large.

Like Joseph who lived very many years before him, Mandela used his success to bless the world in which he lives. His exemplary work including setting up the truth and reconciliation Commission in South Africa demonstrates that life is truly about 'today' and sorting out problems and then moving forward, rather than about looking or moving backwards, blaming other people or yourself, or staying in the past.

One of the remarkable success stories that I remember being told as a young child in primary school was the story of Florence Nightingale, 'The Lady with the Lamp'. She did nursing at a time when it was not considered a suitable career. Her parents did not even allow her to become a nurse. The doctors and male nurses resented Florence when she helped to treat wounded soldiers during the Crimea War around 1853. But because she knew her mission and enjoyed what she did and did what she enjoyed, the wonderful Florence gave up giving up and helped to establish nursing as a dignified and respectable profession.

Mary Seacole whose mother was Jamaican and father Scottish was blocked from going to the Crimea when she also volunteered to help out there because she was a Black person. Like Florence Nightingale, she gave up giving up because she knew her mission. Mary Seacole went to the Crimea anyway, established a hospital there and saved many lives.

Statements such as 'it's a man's world' or that you have to be of a particular sex, race, colour, intelligence level or whatever else is used to categorise people in order to succeed in life are definitely not true.

The Ratified Evidence About Life has shown that by getting real and then driving their personal success programmes forward through their own personal courage and determination, women have risen to various high positions in the world at large and achieved remarkable successes in various areas of life in a so-called man's world.

Similarly, the Ratified Evidence About Life has also shown that regardless of their sex, colour, age, marital status, disability, and so on, various people have become remarkable success stories and number one in their own worlds through getting real.

Success is the birthright of people who get real. Regardless of your background you are guaranteed to succeed in life when you get real. **This world is a real world in which real people who get real succeed**.

GUARANTEED SUCCESSFUL JOURNEY

When you travel by any means – road, air, sea, and so on – you can never guarantee that your journey would be successful.

Understandably, the success of such journeys can never be guaranteed because the Ratified Evidence About Life has shown that anything could happen when we travel. The reality of life is that when we travel by any means in life, there are things that could happen on our journeys that might terminate our journeys or even terminate our lives.

The reality of life has also shown that when we travel on the road to success various things could happen also; for example, you might miss your target, you might face different obstacles, you or other people could let you down, you might sometimes feel discouraged, and so on. However, like the sun that is guaranteed to shine, you can guarantee that you would personally successfully travel on the road to success by getting real.

Whenever I am travelling on any road and I see the sign 'Road Works', it reminds me that the road to success in life is truly tough and that only tough people who can properly, actively, persistently, and skilfully carry out the works necessary to make the road to success passable actually succeed in life.

A crucial thing that we must all learn and DO based on the lives of successful people is that they all had a dream and they all actually successfully achieved their dreams by DOING things that guarantee success.

DOING is something that helps you on the road to success. You must work hard and work well on the road to success in order to enjoy the benefits of successful living!

The road to success is about works. When you *get real* and tackle the works on the road to success you would find a way to succeed and you would definitely succeed and continue to succeed in life.

This is the evidence that comes from life. And like the sun, it is the evidence about life that would remain forever. Even if failures in life try to eclipse this evidence with any contrary view, the

*R*atified *E*vidence *A*bout *L*ife would shine; and it would shine forever.

I wish for you to have a big dream and to turn your dream into reality. I also wish for you to remember to celebrate success by being a blessing to yourself and the wider world in which we all live. I further wish for you to remember never to be arrogant or pompous just because you are successful. We are all 'better at' different things and nobody is 'better than' another. Different people succeed in different areas of their own lives. Our common goal in life is to be number one in our own personal worlds and succeed in various areas of our own lives.

You should activate your dream TODAY. Like the sun, you can shine always and please DO; shine on yourself and the wider world around you. The fact that we are all human beings does not mean that everyone would succeed in life because success comes only through HUMAN DOINGS.

> ... *I did not receive it from a human source, nor was I taught it, but I received it through a revelation...*
> (Galatians 1:12)

It gives me great pleasure and joy that I have revealed to you the real secret of success. I wish for you to GRASP that revelation. To GRASP the real secret of success means to:

Get
Real
And
Succeed
Permanently.

Remember: Like the sun that shines permanently, you too can have a *place in the sun* (that is, you too can succeed in having a prominent and favourable position in life) and permanently shine on your own life and on the lives of other people around you.

The conclusive and *R*atified *E*vidence *A*bout *L*ife reveals that life is a journey which all human beings get in and get out; but not all human beings get on.

The only way to identify, understand and then DO the things that would enable you to permanently *get on and succeed* in life is to GET *REAL*!

ABOUT THE AUTHOR

Dr Innocent Izamoje

Innocent is the Managing Director of On Top Consulting Limited, a training and management consultancy company that works with individuals and organisations helping them to get to the top and be number one in their own worlds by enabling them to get real. As well as having worked with numerous individuals and organisations, he has also presented national and international events.

Innocent is a very experienced, practical, and inspiring motivational speaker, management and personal development trainer and consultant. He combines a wealth of practical experience with knowledge and skills gained from working in a gentle, down-to-earth and supportive way with a wide variety of people and organisations.

Innocent's special and heartfelt passion is to assist people to get real, be number one in their own personal worlds, fulfil their destinies in life, and make the world a better place to live. He believes that everyone can and should succeed in life. He likens life to a cake: various ingredients that blend with each other are required to properly put it together; it comes in different sizes, shapes and colours; you enjoy it and happily share it with other people.

Innocent lives in London with his wife and children.

YOUR COMMENTS

We welcome feedback from readers who personally wish to comment on any aspect of GET *REAL*!

The book was written out of a heartfelt desire to help you get on with successful living. It contains examples of the application of the real secret of success and how people turn their lives into a remarkable success story, a blessing to themselves and other people.

We would be very happy to know that you have found the book helpful and useful. If so, and you would personally like to motivate and bless other people through sharing your success story with them, then please write to us with your comments.

We appreciate and thank all those who personally wish to comment on any aspect of GET *REAL*! Please send your comments to us at the E-mail address on the back cover of this book.

If you personally wish and authorize us to publish your comments, we would be pleased to consider them for inclusion in our published material(s), royalty-free, and without any form of obligation other than assigning your own comments to you in the way you instruct us.

In line with the principles of respecting your choice and confidentiality regarding the protection of your identity where private or intimate experiences are reported, please let us know how you would like your comments to be assigned; for example, a comment by Innocent Izamoje who resides in London, United Kingdom could be assigned to him if he so chooses as (a) "Innocent Izamoje, London, United Kingdom"; or (b) "Innocent, London, United Kingdom"; or (c) "I. I. London, United Kingdom".

NOTES

NOTES

NOTES

NOTES

NOTES